CAPITAL PUNISHMENT PATHOLOGY: THE CASE FOR RESTORING HANGING AS THE METHOD OF EXECUTION

BY

RHETT TORR RIQUE

Capital Punishment Pathology: The Case for Restoring Hanging as the Method of Execution

by Rhett Torr Rique

Library of Congress Cataloguing-in-Publication Data

Note: In academic writing the convention is to cite references in the text or a footnote, by author or lead author and publication date (i.e., Smith, J., 2025), which in turn refers to the alphabetical list of sources at the end of the paper or book (bibliography), where the complete title and publication information for the reference are given. I used that method for this work. Lead author is given and page references were omitted in the expectation all or almost all readers will access the literature via the internet. The fact that I have cited any book or paper listed does not imply the author(s) either support or oppose any content of this work and they should be consulted directly for their viewpoint, if any. Any perceived innuendo or implication that the following content refers to any individual or entity not identified in the text or citations is purely coincidental.

Table Of Contents

Introduction

An oddity of the debate and discourse over the death penalty is the phrase "humane death" which has been used from time to time to advocate various new methods of state killing, including the latest method of lethal injection. The phrase has been applied to other "modern" methods of killing the condemned, in their hay-day, both the electric chair and gas chamber. As pointed out by Gerber & Johnson in *The Top Ten Death Penalty Myths* regarding lethal injection, the reality is there is nothing humane about an execution– that is, a legally sanctioned killing by a government entity as a criminal or military penalty. The taking of life is essentially the opposite of humane– which means showing compassion or benevolence. Animal rescue organizations favor this term, for example, because they purport to organize compassion for 'unfortunate' animals. Mixing such a term into discussion of the legal sanction of death is odd, a little like the odd reality that humane organizations are forced to euthanize far more strays than they can place as rescue animals.

What humane should mean in this context is not compassion or benevolence, but a purpose to cause death rigorously and professionally, without causing unnecessary or excessive pain or mutilation. That is essentially how the U.S. Supreme Court has defined 'usual and un-cruel' punishment. But this is not news. Since about 1870 there has been an official sentiment to avoid imparting excess pain and suffering by applying scientific methods to state killing out of the eye of the public. This initially was focused on modifying the technique for hanging to make it quicker at killing. But hanging was eclipsed by technology, the electric chair and gas chamber after 1900 in U.S.A.. In the last two decades of the 20th Century lethal injection became the legal method of choice. The idea in deploying this new technology was to make the process of state death objective and modern by contrast to the traditional use of public displays of painful death to terrorize a pre-literate populace into obedience. Jesus's crucifixion, truth told, was routine Roman penology. One result of that change was moving executions into prisons and out of public squares by the mid-19th Century in England and many U.S. states.

Although hanging is now regarded as more or less obsolete as a method of state killing in U.S.A., it is very much still a favored means of execution world wide. Most notoriously in recent history, Saddam Hussein, the Iraqi dictator, was executed by hanging. His hanging using the British long drop method resulted in a quick death. As this goes to press, Bangladesh, in the Commonwealth tradition as formerly part of India, is preparing to execute as many as ten former officials by hanging for war crimes committed during their civil war for independence from Pakistan.

Any discussion of hanging in U.S.A. has to account for lynching and "strange fruit" (from the Billie Holiday lyric), that racial factor that inheres in any account of execution by hanging. Lynching by mobs was a feature of American life from the Revolutionary War. There are several good historical works that deal specifically with this topic included in the bibliography. Precise statistics from the 19th and early 20th Century are hard to compile but the consensus seems to be, as horrific as a lynching is, outside the 'Confederate South' there were far fewer black lynchings than white lynchings overall in U.S.A..

Yet the concentration of lynchings in the former Confederate South following the Civil War is another matter. After Union occupation ended during the Reconstruction Era (as Nicholas Lemann detailed in *Redemption*) lynching became a tool for suppression of negro freemen's civil and economic rights, and that made lynching a symbol of racial oppression.[1] As Marquart, Ekland-Olsen and Sorensen pointed out in *The Rope, the Chair & the Needle*, in Texas the rate of 'spontaneous' lynchings did not abate until about 1924 when jurisdiction for executions was taken from the county level to the state level, and death was administered by electrocution in the state's single electric chair. Bitter though black history may be after emancipation, there is a big difference between "hate" executions (lynching) and state executions for crime following a trial under modern jurisprudential standards.

Nor was the "Wild West" as the later American Frontier came to be known, nearly as rowdy and lawless as fictional accounts would have it. One of the first things miners did in Montana, Colorado and California was to organize themselves into that kind of local political unit known as a *mining district* in order to keep track of claims, try to keep the assayer honest, and establish law and order. Despite the movie portrayals, Abilene and Dodge City were not cowboy destination resorts; they were rail head and stockyard complexes for transhipment of cattle to urban markets. Bankers and brokers transacted the 'real' money-- the bars and brothels on the 'Texas' side of the tracks were never more than an economic sideshow. Stripped of romantic ideation and legends, the Gunfight at the OK Corral was about law enforcement taking back control of the streets. In about 40 years of the Territorial Era west of the Mississippi River, there were about 271 legal executions by hanging, compiled by R. Michael Wilson in *Encyclopedia of Murder and Execution in the Wild West.*[2] Meaning the Wild West was more orderly and hangings were far less common than popular media accounts imply and movies dramatize.

Just the same, "extra-judicial executions" were known throughout U.S.A., not just in the so-called Deep South. White hobos and drifters were lynched in California in the 1930's and blacks were lynched in Indiana and other states outside the "cotton belt." Not to imply it was 'better' I am willing to posit that far more blacks were beaten or shot to death than were ever lynched during the terror of post-reconstruction or the Jim Crow era, if only because it was less conspicuous. Nor can all or even a majority of lynchings reliably be attributed to the Klu Klux Klan in the South, as Eliza Steelwater pointed out in her anti-death penalty work, *The Hangman's Knot.* Portraying what was essentially localized white neighbor against black neighbor violence motivated by local animosities, in an era of limited mobility before 1940 in the Deep South, as systematic and coordinated stretches both the facts and the competence of the 'white line.' In a sense, it gives the white terror a 'second wind' of intimidation by "cred." Not until after the technology of mobility and communications made it feasible, and a systematic and coordinated multi-state civil rights movement under the leadership of the Rev. M. L. King began, did the South itself 'rise' in 'caste-based' opposition to integration– and tasted defeat again in the political and legal sense.

In short, there is a lot of 'rural legend' to popular beliefs about lynching. Past lynching of blacks is not a reason in itself to reject hanging as a method of execution. Indeed, the "popular justice" of a vigilante hanging, let's say in the Montana gold fields over theft of a mule by a pair of 'Hibernian japes' who couldn't read what they thought was a receipt, after a 'shout-it-out' trial in the mud caked streets of a tent city, was a mimicry of official 19th Century justice, not something invented on the spot to terrorize a minority. Just the same there is a racial implication in the use of hanging as a method of state killing that has to be respected, and I acknowledge it.

Just as has been done in building a case for de facto or institutional racism under *Brown v. Board of Education* by use of race based statistical analysis in the educational system, a case has been made against the death penalty since the 1970's based on an alleged race bias against blacks and hispanics, among others, in the criminal justice system. The contention is death sentences are meted out to minorities (and blacks in particular) disproportionately. I can understand the argument and can see the 'germ or better' of truth in the raw statistics offered in support.

But there is a cautionary tale. Even if ignorance, oppression (overt or institutional), drug dependency, a 'sub-culture' of despair and cycle of poverty might have a role in shaping crime statistics, there are many examples of heinous and well proven acts of violence by blacks against blacks or hispanics against hispanics, in U.S.A that militates against any form of blanket excuse based on skin color. Infra-community crime rates offer strong reasons against any form of 'get out of death row free' card based on race or ethnic background, poverty, or other alleged environmental determinants of behavior. In short ethnic communities are not trapped in a sort of Skinnerian Box pre-conditioned by "whitey" to submit to servitude, endure poverty, and harm thy neighbor for drugs.

Perhaps the 'iconic cliche' today is the black street corner 'drug thug' killing a bystander shooting at a rival 'drug thug' with a stolen semi-auto pistol, in the words of E. Presley, "down in the ghet-to." Cliche or not, that thug loads his 'heat' with 12 soft-point rounds, one at a time, meaning to do harm with each one, "If that punk shows up again." For that reason there is no defense in, "I didn't have nothing against Mrs. Xampl. I didn't mean to shoot her. I didn't even know she was over there." The statistics that count here are the hundreds of men and women 'Xampls' in that 'hood who aren't packing an attitude and heat, who are instead coping with the selfsame milieu as our urban legend thug, but holding down jobs and keeping their families together. Thug has always had a choice; the subsidized bus or street car fare out of the 'Skinnerian Box' is about $1.90.

Real life is far worse than such discourse. Alton Coleman and his accomplice, Debra Brown, engaged in a tri-state murder 'spree' in 1984, that resulted in death sentences for both– Coleman and Brown were black. Here are some statistics about their many

8

black victims: Vernita Wheat age 9, raped & strangled; Tamika Turks age 7, sexually assaulted & strangled; Donna Williams age 25, raped & strangled; Rachelle Temple age 9, raped & strangled; Toney Storey age 15, raped & strangled. Tamika's relative Annie Turks, age 9, survived and related that after witnessing the assault on Tamika, she was forced to perform oral sex on both Coleman and Brown, violently raped (with lacerations so deep her intestines bulged into the vaginal vault), and was then strangled until she passed out. The point that justice is served by evidence adduced at trial showing guilt or innocence, and not by inferences from statistics, is dangerous to blunt.

I can say with 100% confidence that statistics do not provide even slight protection from the predators on the street in the midst of Black or Hispanic communities, nor any ethnic community. I can also say with 100% confidence there is no mention of race in Matt.13:18-23. And I have never met a person of color who, regardless of his or her beliefs about race or distrust of the "white man," embraced everyone in their community with unguarded *agape*. For these reasons the death penalty serves the interests of communities of color as much as the greater society and for the same reasons. And this book is meant for each and all, co-equally and collectively, of all races and ethnic backgrounds of self-identity.

That said, Debra Brown's death sentence was commuted to life in prison by an outgoing white Ohio governor opposed to the death penalty (and whose sexist actions released all females from death row but only two men). Brown remains in prison in Ohio but is under sentence of death in Indiana. Alton Coleman was executed in Ohio by lethal injection.

What this book is not is a discussion of the "moral" or "human rights" aspects of state killing. There are hundreds of titles in print dealing with these issues but in the end they all boil down to two basic propositions against the death penalty– it is against morality (God's Law) or it is contrary to the social contract (J. J. Rousseau's Law). In my view, very little new or original has been added to the debate since Beccaria's 1764 *Essay* on the one hand, [3] and the verses of the Christian Bible at Genesis 9:6, on the other. Given the debates over the death penalty and seeming perpetual delays of executions, Beccaria's point the deterrent effect of punishment lies in assured and swift consequences is ironic.

This book deals with the merits of hanging as a method of state killing, not the merits or demerits of state killing as a governmental policy. What this book does is address the merits and demerits of hanging in relation to other methods of state killing and argues that– as updated by modern understanding– the traditional common law hanging is the faster and more efficient method of state killing and therefore is one 'best' candidate to be reinstated for the death penalty as an alternate or even primary means.

That is not to denigrate the moral dimension of the death penalty. It is a matter of great social and political importance to make well considered governmental policy if state killing is to be a penalty for crime. But this is not a book that tries to settle the moral issue nor the political issue one way or the other. This book is about the technical advantages of hanging as a method of state killing. With the exception of a discussion of the medical dispute over lethal injection in Chapter 4, which bears on the efficacy of that mode of death, this book leaves the 'whether, who and why' of state killing to those many, many books already out there that cover the subject in abundant detail.

However, to lighten the 'moral' load, the author strongly recommends a critical viewing of three very entertaining films which both educate and dramatize the principal policy arguments around the death penalty, two Westerns and a crime drama. The first is a classic silver screen morality play, *The Oxbow Incident* (20th Century Fox 1943; Henry Fonda; Dana Andrews; Anthony Quinn). The second is the Clint Eastwood film, *Hang 'Em High* (MGM 1968). And the third is a Liam Neeson film, *Under Suspicion* (Columbia 1991). The plot and theatrical dialogue of *The Oxbow Incident* dramatizes the anti case with thespian *angst*. *Hang 'Em High* has a scene which illustrates one of the drawbacks of unprofessional hanging (Eastwood's character survives dangling from a tree) and features a replica of a state-of-the-art 19th Century multi-gallows that served real life Judge Parker in the Arkansas Territory back in the day. *Under Suspicion* is a murder mystery set in England and contains several scenes of the gallows and trap door at the Old Bailey in London. Mr. Neeson is cast as an anti-hero in this whodunnit-- I will only give away the plot twist pivots on misdirected humanism, or did it? For extra credit, you can also view the classic "spaghetti western" *The Good, The Bad and The Ugly* (Grimaldi Productions 1966), in which the late Eli Wallach as Tuco and Clint Eastwood as Blondie starred as a sort of odd couple– with Tuco sporting a hemp collar for the neck-tie party.

My personal position on the death penalty is a simple matter of common sense. There are individuals in society who demonstrate by their actions that they pose so great a risk to society that they must be killed by the state for the protection of the public. Life sentences entrain a latent risk to society of escape, commutation or medical or age release (to clear cells and save cost of incarceration but ironically referred to as a 'humane release'), or release in error, with potential commission of further crimes, plus an ongoing risk to non-violent prisoners and guards during a life sentence.

The bad example is the chilling case of Charles Campbell, imprisoned for rape, but paroled in error. Once he was out he went AWOL from a half-way house, hunted down and murdered his accuser, the neighbor who came over to see what was wrong, and the accuser's 9 year old daughter. [4] A life sentence is a lifetime of waiting for this kind of 'opportunity.' And it is repugnant to me to pay the cost of living of such an individual for life– it mocks the law abiding working men and women who must earn their own bread and insults the public welfare since there are not enough public resources to go around for the down and out and out of work in society who are law-abiding despite misfortune.

The issue of pain is also a matter of common sense. There is no way to end the life of a sensate organism without causing some degree of pain. The issue is, if state killing is to occur, was the method chosen a method of least practical suffering? In his book *From Noose to Needle*, referring to the observations of the attending physician at the hanging execution of Wesley Dodd in 1993 in Washington state, who found no pulse but observed slight movement after Dodd was hung, Timothy Kaufman-Osborn poses the question (p. 125): "What, though, is to be made of those faint efforts at inspiration?" This book applies the medico-scientific logic of parsimony to that question and answers: It was not an 'effort;' it was a post-mortem reflex. This book further shows Dodd's death was far swifter than death by the electric chair, gas chamber or lethal injection would have been, with far less inferred physical suffering than those methods– and far more 'humane' than the deaths of the three children he killed.

The argument that state killing costs more than a life sentence is in large part an artifact of "spreadsheet games" with statistics and inflated assumptions about the cost of capital appeals on which the claim is based, that are not 'facts.' There is even a sort of 'feedback loop' in the legal dithering over carrying out a sentence of death that self-generates much of this alleged cost. The cynical tendency to appoint retired former prosecutors to appeal death cases entrains an incentive to 'paper' every conceivable legal argument against execution as an (oft-alleged meager) supplement to their retirement pay. At any rate, the actual price of hanging a prisoner is far less than any other method– there is plenty of 3/4" rope around and the power source is gravity.

My ideas about this subject shifted with an image of a child's bones found in the incinerator at the cabin where Charles Ng and Leonard Lake conducted torture murders of men, women, and children. The bodies were dismembered with a bloody rack of tools and disposed of in a makeshift oven at their 'personal sized Auschwitz' in the Sierra Nevada foothills in Calaveras County, California. The child may be the child of one of the women whose torture was videotaped at the site, with a child's cries heard in the background. Lake poisoned himself when caught; Ng was convicted of torture murder and sentenced to death in 1999.

In my view, the only unresolved issue in Ng's case is the procedural and fiscal torment imposed on the State of California and Orange County where he was tried, that kept him in center stage of a media drama for years and cost over $20 million dollars. Ng's trial was one of the World's Greatest Death Penalty Circuses in history, only topped in recent times by The Mistress of Murder Show, starring and directed by Jodi Arias. [5] Ng sits on death row to this day, and his costs go up and up.

Also in my view, if sensate experience of the condemned is the constituent of cruelty in the legal phrase "cruel and unusual" then the sensate experience of the victims expressed in the silent screams between the lines of the coroners' reports, or audible screams in 'snuff' video tapes, and similar evidence from capital cases around the country, ought also to carry great weight in the policy debate over state killing.

A pseudonym was used for this book in part because of the 'emotional enthusiasm' with which some pursue the goal of abolishing the death penalty, and the fact there are uncharged alleged accomplices of persons mentioned in this book that remain at large in the preposterous extremity of due process death penalty cases routinely are. That is an artifact in California and other states in U.S.A., in the author's opinion, of a credulous, naive, but powerful anti-death penalty lobby. If it were up to me, I would "rub the noses" of some zealots in the stench that rises when a coroner opens a body bag with remains recovered from the roadside brush or a backyard grave. That would serve as a mnemonic to temper what I consider an immature tendency at times by the anti-death penalty lobby to try to 'win' what is not a game as if it were a political game.

As suggested above, I am not unmindful of the moral arguments. But I consider the primary moral issues to be a matter between the condemned prisoner and his or her spiritual advisor, if he or she has any spiritual beliefs. At common law the *ordinary* (clergy) was always provided at the scaffold to encourage and witness a prisoner's repentance or take his or her confession. If repentance was sincere and heartfelt, the trap door became the gateway to Paradise. But the sentence was carried out regardless since an execution is Caesar's business. The issues of mercy and forgiveness were then and still are today, matters best left to a Higher Power by the government agents charged with protecting the public.

Rhett Torr Rique, Claro Vista, CA, U.S.A.

---

[1] Jack Schuler, in *The Thirteenth Turn*, an anti-death penalty work, referred to the surge in number and frequency of lynchings in the Confederate South as an 'epidemic' between 1888 and 1930.

[2] The statistics compiled on the "Espy File" website may conflict with this but are hard to interpret since they cite executions by state and are not broken down for territorial status; approx. 4000 total is given for all U.S. 1850-1900; http://www.deathpenaltyinfo.org/executions-us-1608-2002-espy-file.

[3] Beccaria 1775; Ch. 28 is the origin of the imprisonment is more effective than capital punishment contention. Beccaria's work is philosophical not statistical or empirical.

[4] The child's throat was cut so deeply she was almost decapitated; the coroner reported there was so little blood left in her veins he had trouble taking a blood sample. Medically that meant her vital child's heart raced to try to cope with anoxia and pumped her circulatory system dry through the severed carotid arteries. It is uncertain if Campbell forced the mother to witness the daughter's murder before the mother died. God's mercy may be infinite but that's not a reason to impose 'calculated' secular risks on any community. Campbell was competently hanged for his murders; his race is irrelevant, a 'null set.'

[5] You got to give Jodi credit– she spent the state's bankroll and beat the death penalty.

[6] Formalized by the Capital Punishment Amendment Act of 1868 in England. In U.S.A. this trend coincided with a surge in anti-death penalty sentiment c. 1840. Flanders 1991; Masur 1989. And by 1865 the Lincoln conspirators were hanged inside a military prison despite public outrage.

Chapter 1:

De-Mythifying Death

There's no denying it: Death by hanging meant strangulation for several centuries of its history and into the 20th Century. The Romans, the Angles and Saxons who brought the custom to England with their two-post *gallows*, and later in the several *civitates* of Europe, typically used a cord and a slip knot to hang the condemned. The use of a temporary *scaffold* or special purpose fixed *gallows* are relatively late innovations, such as the notorious "tree" at Tyburn Hill, a crossroads once on the rural outskirts of London, England. The Tree was a triangular gallows with three sturdy cross-beams used for executions from 1571-1783 A.D. It was so arranged so that three gallows carts could be driven underneath all at once– an efficiency of scale you might say.

The more common method across Europe was use of a simple post with a short length of cord attached near the top. The condemned was obliged to step up onto a box or stool, the noose was slipped over the head, and then the foot support kicked away by the executioner. The result was what became known in the 18th Century as a short drop, which does not break the neck and instead strangles the condemned when the knot slips to the back of the neck and the cord or rope tightens. It was common well into the 20th Century to grab the legs and pull or push down on the shoulders of the condemned to force the ligature tighter if needed to hasten death using the short drop. This technique for hanging is still in use (or at least potential use) in Eastern Europe and the Balkans, the Near East and parts of Far East Asia. Among the illustrations is a photo of Balkan troops carrying out what appears to be reprisal against partisans, in which the short drop post and ligature method is used. This method using a cord garrotes the condemned.

The horror of the idea of strangling to death is likely at the root of much of the bad official reputation hanging accumulated over time, even if hangings were popular community events "back in the day." Executions were once thought to be a necessary public spectacle, especially in the pre-literate era when the public had to be shown justice was done and news of the doings in cities traveled by word of mouth to the countryside. The sight of the condemned twisting at the end of his rope no doubt made an impression. But that was not the only negative– decapitation became a persistent problem for the hangman in the era of the long drop in the 19th and 20th Centuries, and again in 2007 during an Iraqi execution of a war criminal. Often the 'unsightly' or 'vulgar' secondary aspects of death by hanging, such as the "death kick" and other convulsive movement or defecation, associated with the short drop, were believed to indicate a slow death and helped to bring public hangings into official disrepute in England and U.S.A..

But the primary factor causing adverse sentiment in England and U.S.A. was a consensus among the merchant and middle class that, so far from sober and cautionary, public hangings had become almost festive spectacles, notoriously an excuse for "the mob" to drink alcohol that brought out hawkers and pickpockets "in droves," not to mention fostered superstitions such as that the touch of someone hanged was curative, that could cause a rush to the gallows afterward. That antipathy brought sentiment for reform and executions were brought within the walls of prisons by mid-19th Century where executions are performed by prison staff or sometimes a contract executioner, in a more somber and ceremonious way, out of sight of the public today. [6]

As will be discussed in detail in a later chapter, the correct or proper objective of a modern execution by a *calculated drop hanging* is to break the neck, severing the spinal cord, and causing a near instant death, although in practice it is more likely the constriction of the *ligature* (noose) causes *global ischemic anoxia* as the primary cause of death, with secondary cervical trauma at C1-C2. The principal point of this book is such a death is far preferable– in the sense of efficient and quick– for the government as well as the prisoner, than the electric chair (cooks the flesh until cardiac arrest occurs), gas chamber (causes caustic pulmonary edema secondary to chemical anoxia), or lethal injection (a mix of chemicals that paralyze the diaphragm preventing breathing and induces a heart attack), all of which methods can take 20 minutes or more to work despite all being a result of 'enlightened modernization.'

By contrast, done competently, a hanging renders the condemned insensate in less than 15 seconds, and causes complete stoppage of cardio-pulmonary function within six minutes and is thus far less traumatic to the prisoner. Brain death occurs before ultimate cardiac arrest, after the falling body is arrested by the rope and tight constriction of the arteries and veins in the neck by the noose stops blood flow into or out of the head, even assuming the spinal cord is not compromised. It is true that, even if all is done correctly, there may still be some convulsive movement. But since the condemned is already 'brain dead' it is not a struggle for life– that's the first myth to be dispelled.

By contrast, during the old short drop method of hanging execution that induces *asphyxia* (strangulation) because of partial constriction of the rope or cord, the condemned then has a series of convulsive neural responses or 'struggles' of chest heaving, 'thrashing' and kicking. The many stories of the condemned surviving a hanging can be attributed to a lack of adequate constriction to cause death. By contrast, very few if any ever walked away from a competent long drop hanging, including in 2007 Saddam Hussein, the former Iraqi dictator.

Surprisingly, despite its long history, the actual cause of death by hanging was a matter of limited medical investigation (principally by 18th & 19th Century anatomists 'hungry' for specimens from the gallows), and much more 'lore and legend.' But in the 20th and 21st Century a body of medical literature was developed by emergency services physicians dealing with neck trauma, initially because of the need to treat cervical fractures caused by auto accidents. Indeed the medical term *hangman's fracture* derives from this literature, not the penal system. The result was a four part system for of commonly seen fractures and fractures with displaced vertebrae (*subluxation*) in emergency treatment. [7]

But because hanging is also very 'popular' method of *self-homicide* (suicide) it is a relatively common emergent medical crisis. And there are a persistent number of genuinely accidental strangulations where rope or cord or cloth becomes wrapped around someone's neck in the workplace or at home. From this need developed medical clinical incentives to describe the injuries that occur during strangulation and in particular the sequence of medical events that lead to death by strangulation during a hanging, in order to develop emergent treatment protocols and recovery regimens. There also developed related medical literature of forensic investigation to determine cause of death in crime investigation, it being common cunning to hide a strangulation or suffocation murder by staging a self-homicide hanging. [8]

This body of medical literature is even more compelling in dispelling the myths about hanging since suicides are almost always a short drop (because the rope is typically attached at only arm's length overhead), and self-homicides often are found strangled with the body partially supported by the feet or other objects. [9] By contrast, its a rare executioner who would fail to have his prisoner 'swing' clear off the ground. In self-homicides, on one hand the short drop effect is something of a self-cruelty in that it prolongs the death process by reducing the constriction of the ligature. On the other hand, it results in many 'failures' where the self-victim survives to live to reconsider his or her impulse.

The same injuries tend to be found in accidental hangings, and especially in autoerotic hangings. [10] In the final scene of *The Good, The Bad and the Ugly*, Tuco would toe the ground if he fell off the marker; partially supported, he would have hung in a manner similar to many suicides or fatal autoerotic hangings, if Blondie missed the rope. So in that sense the medical literature describes what may be the 'worse case' of a prolonged process of hanging, where the ligature does not constrict tightly or tightens in stages.

I have decided to rely principally on one series of medical articles for purposes of describing the medical sequence of events in a strangulation hanging event. These medical papers describe in detail the sequence of events during a short or impeded drop hanging of the type just described because the data was derived from 'raw' or emergent treatment records and covered a reasonably varied sampling. The majority were suicidal hangings, but those are most relevant and analogous to this subject of execution by hanging as a purposeful act. And, for whatever reason, many of the self-homicides and the autoerotic victims filmed their actions and left a record which the medical doctors were able to view and analyze, in order to describe and interpret medically the sequence of events in this type of hanging death event. [11]

First a nontechnical lesson in neurology and anatomy. The human body has two separate systems of nerve 'circuits' the *somatic* and *autonomic*. The somatic system, which controls voluntary movement, is connected to the brain via the spinal cord. The spinal cord is protected by a flexible chain of bones, the C1-L5 sequence of vertebrae held

18

together by ligaments. The vertebrae have a hollow core which forms a tube through which the spinal cord of nerves descends from the brain, and from which various nerve roots 'branch' out to the body, encased in the *thecal sac*. (Imagine an insulated phone cable with side lines branching out left and right to each house along a street.) But some of the major autonomic nerves bypass the spinal cord by 'direct lines' to the brain stem. As is general knowledge, it is possible for the heart to continue to beat and the lungs function even if someone is paraplegic due to a spinal injury or is in a coma and "brain dead." The principal sources of the convulsions and other unconscious bodily movements of a person dying by short drop hanging are nerve impulses from the most primitive parts of the autonomic nervous system. This is the reason that despite the person becoming unconscious during hanging convulsive body movements might continue to occur.

The medically verified trauma sequence for strangulation hanging, referred to as the *agonal sequence*, is as follows: [12]

Loss of Consciousness 10 sec.; Convulsions 14 sec.; Decerebrate [13] rigidity 19 sec.; Deep abdominal respirations 19 sec.; Decorticate [14] rigidity 38 sec.; Loss muscle tone 1 m. 17 sec.; End of deep abdominal respirations 1 m. 51 sec.; Last muscle movement 4 m.12 sec. Since these values were observed despite diversity of circumstances and partial suspension (i.e, feet or knees touching) the results present the observed course of pathophysiology of human strangulation hanging. [15] The second myth dispelled about hanging is thus that death is slow. Death takes less than five minutes even in an 'amateur' hanging when suspended from a ligature with incomplete constriction.

There are two important points drawn from the foregoing. First, loss of consciousness is rapid and, second, muscle contractions (rotation, adduction and constriction) persist for several minutes after loss of consciousness. That is why I conclude that the morbid intuition of the public at public hangings of old, that death was agonizing and prolonged, based on the kicks and other movement of the condemned at the end of the rope, is a myth. Death is actually rapid following loss of consciousness and within four minutes, if not seconds. Brain death is inferred from the loss of muscle tone ('going limp') within 100 seconds; later 'last gasp' convulsions being involuntary autonomic responses even in the partial suspension hangings studied. [16]

This has importance because of the problem of the occasional revival of a condemned person after being cut down or if the condemned did not die after many minutes and was cut down, being offered in opposition to hanging or the death penalty generally. In the Middle Ages and even later into the 18th Century before the long drop was adopted, this was a 'miraculous' event and a tradition existed that the prisoner had to be let go.[17]

One consequence of this was attendance of a physician by the 19th Century to take a pulse and pronounce death, as well as amending the sentence of death to the phrase "to be hung by the neck until dead" instead of "hung by the neck." As a result of these innovations the condemned was left up until pronounced dead. Another result was a medical observation that a heartbeat could sometimes be detected after the 'limp' phase of the above sequence and breathing had stopped. Because brain death is inferred before that point, the heartbeat detected indicated a live body only, in the manner common to coma after traumatic brain injuries if the torso is uninjured. Thus even if death was regarded as final only when the pulse stopped, the condemned would have been unconscious and insensate from brain death well before the pronouncement.

For these reasons, what the audiences of all those public executions of yesteryear saw were spasms originating in the autonomic nervous system that appeared to last longer than the 20 second reality for unconsciousness and 90 seconds to brain death. [18] The third myth of a prolonged death struggle by the condemned strangling at the end of the rope was counterintuitive. Because of the rapid onset of unconsciousness and brain death the execution was not cruel despite the visible convulsions the pre-literate crowd may have believed was the condemned trying to escape the noose. In reality, assuming the rope and knot held and the condemned was left up longer than five minutes or so, he or she was already brain dead as a result of global cerebral ischemia from the constriction of the carotid arteries caused by the ligature and cervical trauma, well before the pulse stopped.

None-the-less the 'unseemly' spectacle of public hangings inspired the Irish and British to put an end to public hangings. During the intermediate phase the wooden gallows with steps leading to the top was adopted in England and copied elsewhere including U.S.A.. But by 1860 the hanging itself was held within the prison walls, to avoid the 'macabre carnival' of a public hanging. In Colonial America a hanging originally had a cathartic effect among the religious communities, with psalm singing and public confession and prayers for forgiveness of the condemned by the Almighty, as if the hanging was a form of services. [19] The practical reality became far less sober, solemn, and religious as the American population grew and more resembled the "holiday" or "game day" atmosphere of English public hangings in which the condemned's spirit was speeded along by copious consumption of spirits. [20]

[7] Generally injury at C2 and C3 cervical vertebrae. Reyes, et al., 2011; Li, et al., 2006 (review).

[8] E.g., Terazawa et al. 1991. See also Pollanen 2001.

[9] Re effect of body posture on constriction of ligature: Khokhlov 2001a, 2001b; re range of injuries: Sharma et al. 2008; Suárez-Peñaranda 2008; re variety of typical 'household' ligatures: Jayaprakash & Sreekumari 2012.

[10] Partial constriction of the ligature is supposed to induce hypoxic ecstacy during masturbation possibly due to baroreflex from pressure on the carotid sinus. This form of sexual self-abuse is known as *erotic asphyxiation*. Famously the actor David Carradine hung himself to death engaging in this practice, deadly to women as well as men if it induces syncope with the ligature in place. See note 93 infra.

[11] Sauvageau, et al., *Agonal Sequences in 14 Hangings With Comments on the Role of the Type of Suspension, Ischemic Habituation, and Ethanol Intoxication on the Timing of Agonal Responses* (Am. J. Medical Pathology, 20/10 2010); see also Sauvageau 2010b; Sauvageau 2009.

[12] Averaged values adapted from Table II in Sauvageau, et al., *Agonal Sequences, op cit.*.

[13] "[T]he patient lies in rigid extension with the arms internally rotated at the shoulders, elbows, knees, and hips extended, and fingers, ankles, and toes flexed. The jaw may be clenched with the neck hyperextended." (Farlex on-line Dictionary.)

[14] "The patient exhibits bilateral adduction of the shoulders, pronation and flexion of the elbows and wrists, and extension, internal rotation, and plantar flexion of the lower extremities." (Farlex on-line Dictionary.)

[15] The observations were made from film or video recordings; thus no final pulse was taken.

[16] This has been referred to in legal proceedings as "decerebrate twitching" (meaning movement without mentation).

[17] In 1650 for example, two days after her hanging Anne Greene was resuscitated on the dissection table at Oxford and her miraculous survival resulted in a pardon. Ropes also broke on occasion. In 2013 a prisoner in Iran cut down after 12 min. survived a 1.3 m. drop hanging (Sabermoghaddam, et al., 2015), but after recovery was ordered back to the gallows for dealing 'crystal' methamphetamine.

[18] The controversy over what is death or, rather, medical death justifying ending artificial life support, is beyond this book. What is meant here is loss of consciousness, cognitive function and voluntary muscle control– sometimes known as *cerebral death*– where autonomic heart beat and involuntary muscle contractions may continue. This condition is also known by the "street terms" of "being a vegetable" or in a "vegetative state" meaning body tissues are alive or kept alive artificially, but without any remaining consciousness due to brain death. The effects of anoxia are covered in Chapters 5 & 6 following.

[19] Masur 1989.

[20] Flanders 1991.

Chapter 2:

A Short History of the Modern

Long Drop Execution

The world is indebted to the English and Irish for the modern, long drop hanging intended to induce a cervical fracture.[21] The essential difference between the short drop and long drop hanging is the difference between strangulation hanging and cervical fracture hanging. The long drop was adopted because it is supposed to result in a more 'humane' death than a strangulation hanging. The idea can be traced to Irish prison authorities who sought to improve the lethality of hanging and avoid decapitations. William Marwood, a 19th Century British executioner picked up on the idea and used it in his work. [22] Marwood developed the first calculated drop table [23] and could be called the first modern executioner even if his ideas may have been borrowed. He was succeeded by one Binns, who by showing up inebriated was blamed for a 13 minute death at his last execution. James Barry then succeeded Binns and although he was competent and used a computed drop table, had two decapitations reported in the press. That prompted the British Home Office, that was responsible for executions, to convene a commission to resolve the problems with the correct drop.

In this era about 1860-1890, the hangman's rope became standardized in England, based on Marwood's design which relied on a brass ring roved into one end of the rope, through which the noose was made instead of using a hangman's knot. This reduced or eliminated any friction as the noose tightened at the end of the drop. Marwood's rope was 10' 2.5" of 3/4" diameter hemp rope. A D-shackle and length of chain was used to affix the rope to the overhead beam on the gallows and adjust it. A lever operated trap door, with hinges and an iron pin, became standardized in the design of the scaffold, an elevated wood-plank platform with steps leading up to a stage below a cross-beam, that was common from about 1818. [24]

Marwood, who was a bootmaker by trade, also designed a leather waist strap that incorporated arm straps, as well as ankle straps, which restrained the condemned during the drop to help insure a 'straight' or feet first fall. The idea of placing the noose to the side is attributed to Marwood, who believed that offset placement helped induce fracture, but it was likely in use well before him. [25] Within the English Commonwealth nations with the common law tradition of execution of the condemned by hanging, such as Australia, Canada, India, Pakistan, Singapore, Kenya & South Africa, Marwood's brass ring noose, rope and restraints were used well into the modern era, until the death penalty was repealed in Britain and elsewhere. As mentioned in the introduction, as this book goes to press, Bangladesh (formerly a part of India) is preparing to execute war criminals from its civil war using this 'Commonwealth' protocol for hanging.

By 1886 James Barry had come up with a new formula for calculating the drop (412/weight in stone=drop in feet), and used a table for his hangings. The Home Office convened what was known as the Aberdare Commission, after Lord Aberdare, its chairman, in 1886 to settle the question of the 'best' way of calculating the drop, based on Marwood's and Berry's tables and Rev. Haughton's formula (drop = 2240/wt. prisoner in lbs.). This was important because the height and weight of the prisoner were variables in what is in effect a math problem of deriving a 'mass times velocity' computation of enough force to snap the neck but avoid using a drop that generates an excess force that could decapitate the corpse. [26] A reduced force of 1000 ftlb. [450 kgf.; 4400 newtons] was proposed to try to avoid decapitations.

Following a series of hearings, a Table was published based on weight and height of the condemned from which the hangman could determine the correct drop. The table was finalized in 1913. And Albert Pierrepoint, perhaps England's last great hangman, during his execution of Nazi war criminals in 1945-1946, reputedly followed Marwood's formula, similar to the Washington State protocol calling for 1250 ftlb. of energy.

The stimulus for the 1913 revisions was in part the medical research of Dr. Frederic Wood-Jones (who examined 100 skeletons from executions by hanging in the Roman era), which revealed a fracture of the base of the skull was the likely cause of death, and cadaver experiments by Dr. de Zouche Marshall. From that point on the intended penal objective of the calculated drop became a fracture. Specifically, the ideal drop from 1913 forward was intended to induce a cervical fracture and spondylolisthesis (displacement) of the C2 or C3 vertebrae, that either severed the spinal cord causing instant death or, in an incomplete fracture and partial dislocation, compressed the spinal cord, causing paralysis and instant death.

The modern British drop table [27] is essentially a method for applying sufficient kinetic force to induce a dislocated C2-C3 fracture and instantaneous 'humane' death. Whether that result was obtained in practical experience or not was never adequately established, thanks in U.S.A. to the shift away from hanging, initially in favor of the electric chair, even before 1913. The rapid shift from hanging to the electric chair or the gas chamber, and most recently, lethal injection, drastically reduced the number of judicial hangings in U.S.A.. More on those topics follows, but the true bio-mechanical and medical reality is: The cause of death in long drop hanging is *global cerebral ischemic anoxia* with cervical trauma.

Yet as Marwood learned over the course of his career with the Home Office in Britain as executioner, placement of the knot and noose was important. By the mid-1800's it was known that the *submental* knot placement (i.e., under the chin) produced a quick death by cervical fracture if the long drop was used. The Irish apparently originally investigated the submental knot c. 1840 because placement of the knot at the back of the head (referred to as *typical*) for short drop hanging caused the rope to cut through the soft tissues if a long drop was used. Putting the knot under the chin transferred the shock-force of the drop to the back of the head, fracturing the vertebrae and causing direct injury to the *medulla oblongata* at the base of the brain. [28]

The difficulty with this placement was the knot was far more likely to slide to the side of the neck than remain under the point of the chin. Marwood simply placed the knot slightly forward (anterior) of the ear, where it tended to end up, which he believed also achieved the result of a fracture. One fellow even came up with a device for holding the knot and rope in place under the point of the chin for a submental execution, that he hoped the Home Office would adopt. But Barry and virtually all other hangmen have used Marwood's *subaural* placement in the belief it reliably produced a fracture. The subaural placement of the knot remains standard. As discussed in a later chapter, the subaural knot placement even with correctly calculated drop, may not as reliably induce the true hangman's fracture as once believed, [29] but it reliably results in the rapid death of the condemned.

In 2013 Kuwait conducted a double execution of a murderer and a child rapist applying the Commonwealth brass ring noose, subaural placement, and long drop from a futuristic steel and aluminum gallows. The executions were videoed and are on line (reader discretion advised): *https://cpnagasaki.wordpress. com/2013/06/18/kuwait*. This provides a "lab" for the lessons of this chapter. The prisoner camera-left is killed instantly at the end of the drop; the prisoner camera-right convulses at the end of the drop (bending from the waist) but also dies within 90 seconds. Post mortem photos show his noose slipped past the ear toward the back of the neck (i.e., toward in the 'typical' location of the ligature in self-homicide), and the leather 'stop' meant to hold the brass ring in place was displaced about 18" above the ring. Despite that, justice was clearly swift for both prisoners.

---

[21] The drop is the distance the condemned falls; after the noose was attached; the measured length of rope formed a loop behind the back curving up to the beam above the trap door in the scaffold, that suspends the prisoner after falling through the trap door until pronounced dead. To prevent entanglement the rope is held up and away by a thread or elastic that snaps on the fall.

[22] Laurence 1960; see Bailey 1980.

[23] Dr. Samuel Houghton independently developed a formula in 1866 he referred to as the "Standard Drop," based on generating 1250 ftlb [572 kgf.; 5600 joules] of energy. Marwood's approach was derived from practical experience but similar as a ratio of weight in stones (stone=14 lb.) to length of the drop.

[24] Laurence 1960.

[25] Engel 1996; Bailey 1989; Pierrepoint 1974.

[26] See note 113 infra, re derived decapitation force in self-homicide autopsies.

[27] A copy is at: *http://www.capitalpunishmentuk.org/hanging1.html#table*.

[28] Laurence 1990; effectiveness of submental placement was demonstrated in a modern era autopsy. Wallace et al. 1994.

[29] The subaural placement reliably induces cervical fracture and vertebral dislocation in calculated long drop hanging, but inconsistently, from C1-C5. E.g., Spence et al. 1999 (archaeological study prison graveyards); Wallace et al. 1994. A well illustrated series of case reports of various cervical fractures and fracture types in clinical setting is: Kinoshita 1994.

Chapter 3:

Controversy at Nuremberg

One of the greatest modern scandals surrounding hanging occurred at the post-WWII international war crimes tribunal at Nuremberg, Germany, when a U.S. Combat Engineer named Sgt. John C. Woods, was given the task of hanging several of the condemned Nazi war criminals in 1946. He was originally assigned to hang Herman Göring (Hitler's Air Marshall and long time political associate), along with Alfred Jodl (Nazi Army Chief of Staff), Joachim von Ribbentrop (Nazi Foreign Minister), Wilhelm Keitel (Nazi Field Marshall), Ernst Kaltenbrunner (Nazi SS General implicated in the death camps), Hans Frank (Nazi governor of Poland implicated in the death camps), Aurther Seyss-Urquart (Nazi governor of Netherlands), Alfred Rosenberg (Nazi politician and racial theorist), Julius Streicher (Nazi racial propagandist), Ernst Saukel (Nazi politician), and Wilhelm Frick (Nazi politician), all vicious racists with the blood of millions of Jews and other "undesirables" on their collective hands. In the case of Jodl and Keitel, you add the lives of a million ordinary *soldaten* sacrificed in1944-45, when Hitler was already known to be mentally incompetent. Göring cheated Sgt. Woods with a cyanide pill the night before his hanging. But Sgt. Woods did dispatch the rest the next day. It was the less than "clean" results of his techniques that created controversy.

Sgt. Woods himself was controversial in that he got the job by claiming he had experience doing hangings after courts martial. He did serve with a unit that worked on prison compounds but his claim to have done 347 hangings at a press conference is greatly exaggerated as applied to his military service. There were only 160 G.I.'s executed between 1942-1961, [30] and of the WWII number, 70 executions were done in England. In Woods's case its an "if any" probability. An oddity is he served in the Navy before WWII, was discharged under a cloud, but later joined the Army shortly before America entered the war. His career ended when he was electrocuted in 1950 in an accident installing cable for an atomic bomb test in the Pacific.

When I say unskilled I mean Sgt. Woods was unskilled at hanging. His carpentry was excellent and in that was the problem. He built 3 gallows, each having the same dimensions and same trap door size, and same height beam for the rope, as specified in the U.S. Army manual. He used a standard hangman's 13 turn slip knot , stretched the rope and used the same size hemp rope each time, likely from the same G.I. spool.

The problem was he followed the U.S. Army's protocol for executions,[31] which specified a fixed length of rope.[32] This process of building uniform gallows in a 'workmanlike' manner created the controversy even if it was proficient carpentry.

Everything worked. The problem, because the rope was uniform in length but the condemned were not and varied in bulk from short and lean to tall and robust, on up to Göring, who had a large frame 'marbled' in fat from luxurious living off his loot. In the event Göring became a burden only to the stretcher bearers. But the rest of Sgt. Woods' flight of hell-bound prisoners caused him grief. The Nazis fell through the trap door under the gallows, which were curtained off with black canvas. Several, including Jodl, were struck by the trap door. This was likely due to a combination of small trap door and, by one account, the rubber bushing breaking off so the door rebounded. Also by news accounts of the day, Keitel took extra time to die and Streicher (after hollering "Heil Hitler!") dropped kicking and struggling; Sgt. Woods and an assistant had to duck under the gallows and pull down on their legs to induce death. The rest died "alright" even if the standard rope length worked more or less by coincidence of height and body weight. [33]

I get the feigned, "Oh, darn!" attitude over it taking extra time I have occasionally seen. But the goal of the Allies at Nuremberg was civilized and righteous punishment to demonstrate the triumph of civilization over barbarity, not to inflict further torment on defeated peoples in a world saturated with war's agony. The French, English and Poles took evidence at tribunals and they also hanged other Nazis. The Russians, for the most part, simply confirmed various Nazis' identity (with help from NKVD "as needed"), and then shot them where found. I'm of two minds about Nuremberg vs. the 'expedited' Russian methods.

By contrast, later on and at other locations in Germany and Europe, the British and Pierrepoint, their expert 'national' hangman, were busy dispatching war criminals with calculated drops and 'clean' cervical fracture kills. Needless to say the British were highly critical of the SNAFU by the Americans. The U.S. Army was not too proud not to learn from our ally. In 1947 the U.S. Army modified its execution protocol for hanging to incorporate the calculated drop method that became the standard several states adopted or adapted for civilian hangings.

There were precedents for the "one length fits all" drop used by Sgt. Woods. The four Lincoln conspirators were hanged on a single beam gallows in 1865 with a 5 foot drop each. The four Haymarket Bombing anarchists were hanged in Chicago in 1887 on a single beam gallows with a 4 foot drop each. These were short compared to the drop used by George Maledon at federal Judge Parker's "fancy" gallows in Ft. Smith, Arkansas Territory in the 1880's. [34] Maledon executed 86 prisoners there using an 8 foot drop. The Army manual directives for greasing the rope with oil or wax to allow the knot to slide smoothly, and pre-stretching the rope by test-dropping a sand bag, may have been his legacy since that was his practice. [35] In 1996, the last domestic prisoner to hang, Billy Bailey, was executed at a Delaware state prison for the shotgun murder of an elderly couple, using a calculated drop; at 220 lbs. the drop was 5 feet.

As mentioned above, if the drop is too long, a decapitation can result. Allegedly because he gained weight while awaiting execution, outlaw Tom "Black Jack" Ketchum famously was decapitated in New Mexico Territory in 1901 when the executioner failed to shorten the drop to compensate for the extra weight. By contrast, for one of the last modern executions in U.S.A. in 1993, Westley Dodd at less than 150 lbs. was given a 7 foot (213.36 cm.) drop in carrying out his execution in Washington State. Later Billy Bailey, as mentioned, at 220 lbs. was given a drop of about 5 feet. See Army DropTable. [36]

Both appeared lifeless to the witnesses after the drop with no visible struggle, but as discussed following, the Dodd autopsy showed the vertebrae were extended but no cervical spondylolisthesis. A second Washington state hanging of Charles Rodman Campbell in 1994 was more problematic. As mentioned in the Introduction, Campbell was a rapist and released by mistake to a halfway house after serving part of a prison term for the rape. He escaped and began a series of revenge murders of his former victim, her daughter, and a neighbor. His former accuser was beaten and revenge raped with a blunt object that pierced the vaginal wall, then was stabbed to death. Campbell is also suspected of killing his former accuser's ex-husband by burning him alive with gasoline although not convicted of that crime. As pointed out, Campbell is an argument for execution.

Dodd chose hanging, but Washington State decided to hang Campbell. He engaged in various acts of passive resistance the day of the hanging, and had to be strapped to a collapse board (to keep him upright). A submental knot was used. Campbell died much faster than his victims, and his autopsy showed he did sustain a cervical fracture and severed spinal cord, despite the "complications" of completing the execution. 'Side-by-side' autopsies that demonstrated the different traumatic effects of the subaural and submental knot placement were done using CT scans and necropsy. [37]

Yet another case which had political overtones because the anti-death penalty lobby in England was starting to gain popular support and she was convicted of murder in a "love triangle" dramatized by the press, was the execution of Ruth Ellis. Her 1955 autopsy after being hanged 'by the Protocol' showed a "classic" hangman's cervical fracture at C2 and severance of the spinal cord. [38]

While it is true that there have only been three executions in U.S.A. since 1977 by hanging, an oft repeated statistic, the reality is that all three were conducted effectively in the British/ U.S. Army Protocol manner, and resulted in a swift death– deaths shorter and with less implied sensate distress than any of the other legal alternatives in U.S.A.. [39]

The pronouncement of death after the drop was at 11 m. for Bailey's execution, 4 m. for Dodd's execution, and 6 m. for Campbell's. However they were medically insensate and brain dead well before the official pronouncement of death based on lack of heartbeat. Dodd had no heartbeat after 1 m. although left up several minutes more. As discussed infra the heart can beat after brain death and death of brain tissues occurs very rapidly from the medical effects of sudden constriction of the veins and arteries of the neck by the noose in a long drop hanging. Death is even faster if the spinal cord is compromised by cervical dislocation and/or fracture, as for Dodd and Campbell.

---

[30] Of those, 2 were carried out by the Air Force. There were none in the Navy. Garland (2014).

[31] U.S. Army 1944 Manual, p. 17.

[32] I was not able to confirm but strongly suspect a fixed length was specified by the Army to avoid the (extra) long-drop problem of decapitation, a persistent problem in executions right up to 2007.

[33] One famous eyewitness news account is *The Execution of Nazi War Criminals* by International New Service reporter Kingsbury Smith, October 16,1946; another account, *War Crimes: Night Without Dawn,* appeared in Time Magazine on October 28, 1946; these are searchable on line.

[34] As mentioned in the Introduction this famous gallows was featured in a movie, *Hang 'em High* starring Clint Eastwood. There is a Park Service reproduction on display at the Ft. Smith visitor center. See it on-line at http://www.nps.gov/fosm/learn/historyculture/gallows.htm

[35] Similar practice was specified by the Home Office instructions for hangmen, updated in 1959, following on the practices of Pierrepoint, Barry and Marwood. See Appendix B.

[36] The 1947 Army Protocol is included as Appendix A. A notorious character named Leuchter (allegedly with neo-Nazi sympathies) performed the calculation for the drop; everything worked as intended and Bailey's death was quick, much quicker than his victims. Bird shot from a shotgun blast causes a gaping but shallow wound in the human body that takes time to bleed out.

[37] Wallace et al. 1994.

[38] Her British autopsy is reproduced at: *http://www.capitalpunishmentuk.org/pmortem.html*.

[39] See Denno 2015; Hillman 1993. Covered in detail Chapters 5, 6 infra.

ILLUSTRATIONS

Short-drop, garrote style hanging somewhere in the Balkans.

Execution of Lincoln conspirators. Original photo A. Gardener.

Franz Strasser on gallows with clergy after Dachau Trials 1946.
His war crime was killing POW airmen.
Note the contrast stain of trap door, per Army manual.
U.S. Army photo/wikipedia commons

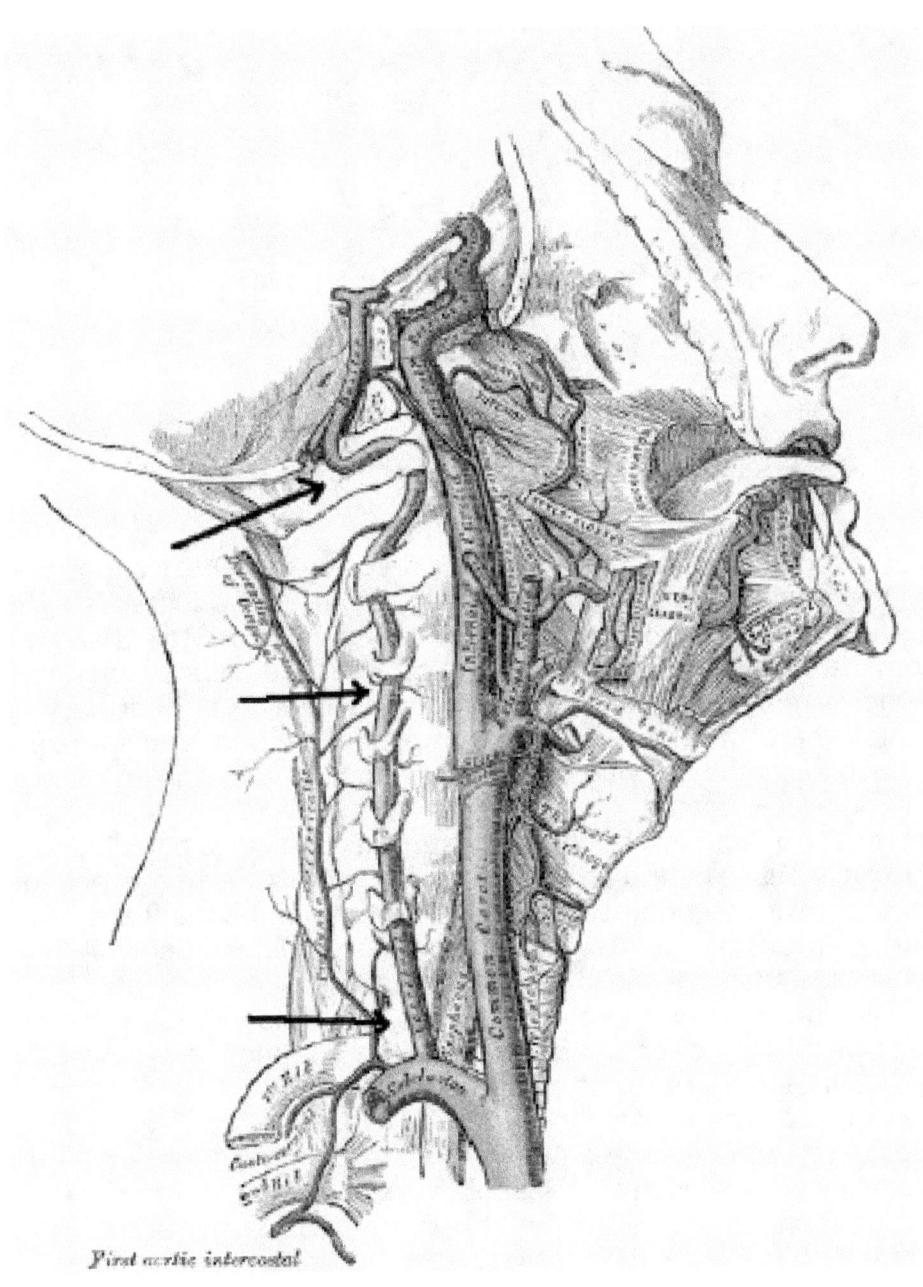

From Gray's Anatomy/wikipedia:

Showing vertebral artery partially shielded by foramen and laying in sulcus on top of C1; note carotid artery and sinus, and source of vertebral artery relative to C6, foramina & carotid artery.

Chapter 4

The Hippocratic Fallacy in Mixing

Politics and Ethics

In medical circles in U.S.A. there arose by the1990's opposition to the death penalty after lethal injection was adopted as the preferred method of state killing, an opposition to what was sometimes called "medicalizing death." The latter expression refers to performing the injection in a room resembling an infirmary or clinic, where the condemned lies on a hospital bed, and someone in a white coat is carrying out the execution by injecting drugs with a hypodermic needle. A lethal injection is a mix of drugs which are intended to induce sequential anesthesia, paralysis, and chemical cardiac arrest to bring about death. The lethal injection execution method was intended to be more humane and satisfy the legal barrier in U.S.A. against "cruel and unusual punishment." A 'raft' of articles soon appeared denouncing medical involvement. [40]

Neither the death penalty or hanging per se have ever been regarded as cruel or unusual under the common law or by the U.S. Supreme Court. [41] In the post-Revolutionary War era, James Mason, in copying "cruel and unusual" over from the English Bill of Rights of 1689 into the new Virginia state constitution, or James Madison borrowing from Mason's version when drafting the 8th Amendment in the Bill of Rights of the U.S. Constitution, most likely had in mind what I call *political spectacle punishments* for crimes against government (e.g., rebellion) that were customary in England from the Medieval period to the 1700's, such as drawing and quartering (so the 'quarters' could be displayed for intimidation farther and wider at separate crossroads than one corpse in the square), breaking at the wheel, the gibbet, burning women for treason, and so on. There is some doubt about the actual English meaning. [42] But there is no doubt neither Mason or

Madison regarded hanging, firing squads, stocks, ducking stools, the pillory, whipping post, branding iron, and other similar rough and common punishments of the Colonial era as unusual or cruel. [43] But by the late 20th Century there was popular sentiment in U.S.A.. to follow the example of other countries such as Britain and ban the death penalty, based on a non-technical claim all state killing was cruel and unusual and imprisonment was adequate punishment.

The general medical negativity over lethal injection was to the impression created by the setting that implied lethal injection was an approved medical procedure. But the "orchestrated and publicized" opposition was founded more on a political agenda of some doctors to abolish the death penalty. The result has been a round of medical resistence to participation in judicial executions, especially resistance to attending or conducting lethal injection procedures. That, coupled with an 'artificial' shortage of pharmo-chemicals specified by state statute or regulation for the fatal injections, has caused delay or obstructed completion of many death sentences by lethal injection as this book is going to press. [44] In 2015, also as this book goes to press, California approved a single drug lethal injection protocol to deal with the pharmo-foiling tactic.

The opposition is vocal and persistent. Indeed, even physicians who only write on the subject have been subjected to negative peer pressure.[45] As a consequence, physicians or other medical practitioners are guarded in expressing any views on the subject of capital punishment and have been forced to avoid participation in executions by direct threats of professional censure and expulsion from medical organizations here in U.S.A. [46]

There is to my mind a Hippocratic Fallacy that underlies this resistance, since physicians facilitate death in many ways. While the Hippocratic Oath refers to 'do no harm' the reference is in context of therapy and treatment. It bears at best indirectly on a civic duty to supervise a state killing in order to prevent unnecessary pain and suffering to the condemned. The medical profession is not, despite the tenor of medical writing in opposition to the death penalty, a "higher intellectual power" on the legality of state killing. Medical doctors are bound by the majority rule in our democratic society as much as any other segment of the population. The fact a civic duty might be unpleasant or distasteful doesn't excuse the obligation to obey the law or the mandate a verdict of guilt and judgment of death represents. But the point here is, this medical death penalty "sit-down-strike" is a form of political statement, and the threat to withdraw certification of otherwise qualified physicians is a form of overt political coercion.

There is a Hippocratic Fallacy even in the "We are Healers not Killers!" argument that sums up most of the medical ethical writing opposing the death penalty. Not long ago medical ethicist's writing amounted to apologetics in support of assisted suicide or "voluntary euthanasia,"and campaigning for its legalization. One result of this movement was the 2005 Mental Capacity Act in Britain which allows doctors to follow advance "do not resuscitate" (DNR) directives. Physician assisted suicide is now legal in four states: California (in 2016), Oregon, Vermont and Washington. New laws allowing it are pending in several other states. World wide many jurisdictions permit advance DNR and *life-sustaining treatment* (LST) directives authorizing physicians to 'allow' death. [47] I agree with frankness in referring to medically mediated death as a form of euthanasia. [48] How a decision is reached to stop LST with or without an advanced directive can be problematic for physician, patient and next of kin. [49]

But medical supervision of a state killing to minimize the trauma and suffering of the condemned during lethal injection is essentially the same role as medical supervision of a suicide by injection to ensure it is effective and done with a minimum of suffering. The elderly terminal cancer victim may be the preferred, sympathetic 'patient' compared to a condemned prisoner with "blood on her hands" but the concept is the same. And in states where it is legal, I'm very sure very few physicians would approve of a "hands off" proscription by professional organizations that forces inexpert elderly spouses or other relatives to have to handle the lethal injection(s) during assisted suicide all alone, with attendant risks of "botching" the death.

Perhaps even more to the point, doctors routinely engage in "euthanasia by triage" in many contexts, from the battlefield to the ER to allocation of hospital resources in cancer treatment or other terminal illnesses. [50] I find it odd that doctors have no issue with 'going along' with the wishes of an inexpert lay family member, who is persuaded to allow them to stop treatment, and commit a passive medical death. Yet the same doctor can be quite adamant about refusing to assist with a state killing even after an extended legal process has made sure the death is lawful for the state to carry out. Not so many years ago, either alternative was considered unethical on the basis no valid moral difference exists between passive and active medical assistance with death. [51]

A doctor often takes a pro active role in the process of a decision to withdraw life support from a patient. A patient may be terminally ill with a static prognosis or may be a patient who is beyond benefit from any treatment or from any treatment more beneficial than palliative measures (e.g., pain management), or be artificially sustained on a resuscitator or similar machinery. [52] Few doctors find ethical issues in talking a family into withdrawing life support in such contexts. [53] That's not to say medical doctors think in 'lock step' about these topics, typically referred to as ethical or moral "dilemmas" in medical journals. Just the same, doctors have been willing to submit to the political actions of their medical associations in 'forcibly' banning medical participation in state killing, a form of coercion that disguises what is an issue of penal politics as medical ethics. In doing that physicians surrender their right to personal conscience. [54]

And all that is in addition to the unspoken but ever-present undercurrent in medical practice of "euthanasia by coverage" because of lack of insurance and dollar limits on coverage for medical treatment or simple resistance by insurance companies in providing coverage for procedures likely to have problematic outcomes, and even just fiscal 'restraint' because the procedure or medication is expensive. [55] Although it occurs in other medical systems, this is an especial problem in U.S.A., where level of care depends on quality of insurance coverage nine times out of ten, even if the medical staff is competent and motivated. Public hospitals face even worse issues thanks to budgetary encroachment on medical decisions that may result in a shortage of cash for even essential medical services.

The author can speak directly to this problem, enduring a form of medical discrimination because his Medicare coverage is refused by most doctors within his service area forcing him into a commute-to-find-coverage game. And the author has no doubt whatever that "euthanasia by coverage" falls disparately on Medicare patients in U.S.A. because the compensation rates for medical treatment under Medicare are regarded by hospital administrators and many private doctors as not profitable enough to 'err' on the side of life sustaining treatment. [56] Frankly, I feel some trepidation on that account. But as may be obvious in writing this book, that risk doesn't deter me from publishing parsimonious conclusions.

I believe the correct solution is to recognize executions

of condemned criminals will continue. The existing legal process is thorough and for crimes that are heinous or involve multiple victims or both, a sentence of death will be well and truly rendered under the law. And for those reasons the casuistry that otherwise executions may entail unnecessary pain and suffering if not medically attended should be a sufficient reason to override the 'official' medical political opposition to the death penalty. To borrow from the anti-death penalty lobby's drama: If botched executions are barbaric aren't aloof medical 'Alarics' cruel? More than a few jurisdictions agree medical assistance is appropriate to reduce unnecessary suffering to the condemned, in enacting "safe harbor" protections for medical professionals who assist in legal executions. [57]

One response I can anticipate if the current medical 'hell no we won't go' to executions attitude persists, and the current pharmacological opposition that has created an artificial scarcity of the chemicals in the approved lethal injection 'mix' persists, is a switch to other legal methods of execution or to legalize new ones. There is a widespread and dominant public sentiment in favor of the death penalty in 34 states of the United States where it is legal and a strong minority view in favor in the remaining states to provide the incentive. And it is not difficult to come up with alternative drug mixes or methods of execution.

Injection of a large dosage of the clinical standbys lidocaine and fentanyl into the spinal cord at the C2-C3 joint to create a whole body "spinal block" to minimize discomfort of the condemned [58] with a second injection (procaine or more lidocaine) targeting the *sinoatrial* and *atrioventricular* nerve bundles in the heart, to cause cardiac arrest, would reliably induce a quick death. [59] An even simpler "off the shelf" alternative, since most jurisdictions already permit substituting drugs in the lethal injection, would be to use a 'procedure' well accepted by the medical profession and with a long history of use in U.S.A. in end of life therapy. That's to adapt injection of the three drug Brampton's Cocktail for the purpose of state killing, by adjusting the dosages. That idea would likely gain wide acceptance on Death Row, if not in many warden's offices, and tends to meet the 'cruel and unusual' objection head on. And, importantly, either of these procedures could be carried out by an ordinary paramedic, or prison trustees trained to give the injections.

Other simple solutions are possible in legislative response to continued medical and pharmacological "vocal passive resistance." One is what I refer to as the Twenty-Six Cent Solution. That is, to acquire a 5" test barrel machine used in firearm manufacture and automate a procedure where the condemned is strapped into a chair and head harness (with or without anaesthesia) and then the test barrel is used with a timer to fire a pistol round at an approximate 60 degree angle into the base of the skull to strike through the hindbrain upward into the cerebrum. Twenty-six cents refers to the bulk cost of the tried and true .38 Special police pistol round, a cartridge more than adequate for the job. Such a solution will reliably result in instantaneous death. [60] Its drawback is its "messy." That might be mitigated by special loading of a light powder charge and frangible bullet that would penetrate the back of the skull and then break into multiple small fragments expending their energy in the brain tissues without retaining sufficient force to exit the front of the skull. [61] The Twenty-Six Cent Solution is well within the capability of existing technology, indeed, another off-the-shelf technology. And it is no more 'unusual or cruel' than the constitutional execution by firing squad method of several states.

If that sounds too "Wild West" (or maybe "Eastern Front") a form of "laser guillotine" could also be devised using more 'off the shelf' technology. But how much better to adapt existing medical technology to establish a new and least medically intrusive, least traumatic procedure for accomplishing state killing. The medical profession would have to apply itself toward using 21st Century medical technology instead of standing by for use of one of the above cruder alternatives or a redux of the Edwardian techniques for hanging intended to induce a cervical fracture described in this work and that is the next best legal alternative.

An example would be use of the gamma 'knife' radiosurgery (GKR) technique to necrotize brain tissue. The GKR is a computer guided procedure (not an actual knife) for treating diseased brain tissues and is often used as a clinical procedure, which means it could be done in prisons. [62] The medical procedure calls for an emitter generating multiple single beams of radiation that are individually benign, but when focused by the emitter to intersect on an area (a lesion, tumor, or vascular obstruction, for examples) can kill the pathological tissue. The therapeutic intent is to use precise "brain topography" to avoid "collateral damage" to healthy nerve tissue, once a very significant problem in old fashioned 'scalpel and saw' brain surgery. But by use of adjusted dosages of radiation it would be possible to cause necrosis of a transverse 2mm section of the brain stem in an anesthetized subject, say at a point approximately 5 mm above the base of the skull across the stem of the medulla oblongata, within the skull above the foramen magnum, including the basilar artery and vagus nerve. This would accomplish essentially and painlessly the same effect as the bulky Edwardian mechanical-drop gallows "machine" intended to sever the spinal cord with the fractured edge of the subluxed C2 vertebra. And with no visible disfigurement of the corpse, by contrast to the Twenty-Six Cent Solution, or electric chair burns, gas chamber cyanide pulmonary edema, firing squad bleeding, etc..

I realize that will seem a gruesome mis-application of technology in the eyes of many medical people not to mention lay death penalty opponents. But we live in a democratic society in U.S.A.. Unless the accused waives the jury, a jury must decide guilt "beyond a reasonable doubt" and vote unanimously for the death penalty. A death penalty jury must be fairly chosen and reflect the composition of the community where the trial takes place; and opposition to the death penalty is not a valid basis for rejecting a juror. Although the AMA took a position against the death penalty and physician participation as early as 1980, the percentage of the population that supports the death penalty rose afterward, and the majority still favors it. [63] Consistently, the death penalty has been reinstated in several states where it had been banned, such as California and Oregon. That indicates the AMA position is somewhat self-indulgent and self-righteous, given the prevalence of physician mediated legal death world wide. [64]

While I don't mean to imply that Christian texts are the only relevant ethical or religious referents, just the same the familiar Biblical commandment, "Thou shalt not kill" in Leviticus 20:13, is tempered by the next verses which also proscribe "Whoever strikes a man so that he dies shall be put to death . . . ." in Lev. 20:14-16. [65] It is thus abundantly clear that the great and abiding majority in the United States, rightly in my view, favors following the traditional common law principle of imposing the death penalty, at least for 'aggravated' or 'first degree' murder. [66]

The final point in this chapter concerns Dr. Jekyll. Being heir to human emotions and human nature and human error, the medical profession walks the journey of life on the same mundane plane as the rest of us. For example, medical professionals can and have been enraged by jealousy in a love triangle and committed a murder. [67] Physicians can and have been accused of crimes for failure to treat patients, such as for withdrawal of life support or failure to provide emergent treatment [68] as well as in the case of famous Dr. Kevorkian, convicted for providing assistance to patients ending their lives despite it being illegal at the time. Indeed, there are from time to time pathological personalities with sociopathic "tendencies" employed in the medical field, as serial murders of geriatric and pediatric patients using 'locked cabinet' drugs attest. [69]

And there are many cases of criminal treatment activity by physicians who mis-proscribe drugs that can result in doctor 'treated' addictions, as well as death to one or more patients. [70]

For such reasons, it is good to recall that the rationale for capital punishment applies to medical professionals as much as the public at large. In that sense, the AMA and ABA opposition to the death penalty could be said to be self-serving as well as self-indulgent and self-righteous. At any rate, last time I checked, there were very few saints and an oversupply of, well, sentient bipedal primates making rounds.

---

[40] E.g., Zivot 2012; Denno 2007. Zivot argues speciously medical aid for less suffering does not make execution humane from a hidden premise all death is cruel ergo execution is cruel with or without MD. Ethical 'hand washing' devalues suffering to zero for condemned who otherwise might die 'easy.'

[41] The famous 1972 case of *Furman v. Georgia*, despite some of the judge's rhetoric, was based on capital punishment being 'unusual' in the sense it was imposed haphazardly because of lack of judicial standards for imposing a death sentence; later cases upheld the death penalty after judges and juries were given rules to follow that made it 'usual' again in the sense of applying standardized criteria. An irony is the very fact of having scalable culpability ('murder 1, murder 2') ensures death will befall only some.

[42] Granucci 1969. Hanging is not a "punishment of torture" under 8th Am. *Wilkerson v. Utah*, 99 U.S. 130, 135 (1878); *Campbell v. Wood*, 18 F.3d 662 (9th Cir. 1994).

[43] See the Colonial Williamsburg Foundation website. Re old methods of judicial execution in general: Banks 2013; Abbot 1994; Laurence 1960. The Spanish Mule and flogging were still commonplace military punishments during the U.S. Civil War; *e.g.*, for desertion in Army N. Virginia.

[44] Widgery 2015; Denno (2007); also Annas 2008, Romanelli Whisman Fink 2008. Re general history death penalty and lethal injection, Banner 2002; Dow & Dow, eds., 2002. Statistics: Evans 2012.

[45] E.g., Longstreth, et al., 2011, criticising Reyes, et al. 2011, on ethical grounds.

[46] See Sikora & Fleischman 1999, calling for sanctions. The American Medical Association position is against capital punishment and physician participation;

the American Nurses Association position is against capital punishment and nurse participation; the American Board of Anesthesiologists in 2010 threatened to withdraw certification of any physician who participates in lethal injection (i.e., regardless of professional competence). *But see* Groner 2002 (an otherwise 'anti' article) relating a necessary intervention by a physician to prevent misplaced infusion of lethal injection "cocktail."

[47] *E.g.*, Jox Hessler Borasio (2008) (Germany).

[48] Vadász 2010; see Bishop 2006; Brock 1992.

[49] Clarke et al. 2015; Parks & Winter 2009; Drought & Koening 2002.

[50] Guidet et al. 2014; Borosky 2012; Kübler et al. 2011; O'Mahony et al. 2010; Mosenthal et al. 2009; Hemphill & White 2009; Wilkinson 2009; Vincent 1999; List 1997; Teres 1993.

[51] Bishop 2006; Sprung et al. 1997; Kopelman 1985; Johnson 1983; contra Quinn 1987; and see Stanley 1989 (Appleton Consensus).

[52] Re "palliative sedation" end of life treatment: Baumann et al. 2011; Bruce & Boston 2011; Cassell & Rich 2010; Eisenchlas 2007 (review); Morita 2005.

[53] Re "pulling the plug" Padela & Moihiudden 2015; Rady & Verheidje 2014; Chakravarty & Kapoor 2012; Mueller 2009 (T. Schiavo). Re "What is consciousness?" Lotto et al. 2012; Khane & Savelescu 2009; Panksepp et al. 2007.

[54] Where the practice or procedure is legal, medical ethics is a matter for individual conscience. Kadlac 2014; Brock 1992 (p. 123, 129).

[55] Enomoto et al. 2015; Tangka et al. 2015; Hughes & Smith 2014; Blanchette et al. 2008; Payne et al. 2002; Emmanuel 1996; see generally re effect of economics on medical decision making: Orlendahl 2008; Orlendahl Fries 2006; West et al. 2003.

[56] See re public funding cost benefit analysis Kelley et al. 2015; Manchikanti Singh Hirsch 2012; Manchikanti & Boswell 2007; Tappenden et al. 2007; Forbes et al. 2001; and see Tangka et al. 2015; Blanchette et al. 2008.

[57] Sawicki 2008.

[58] Re clinical applications: Förester & Rosenberg 2011; Pollock 2003; Urmey 2003. Intrathecal injection of opiate and anaesthetic 'combo' is the 'classic' labor & delivery 'spinal block' pain relief methodology. E.g., Hamber & Visconi 1999; Lo Chong Chen 1999.

[59] Injection of procaine intravenously is contraindicated and can induce convulsions; that risk is mediated by the dosage of fentanyl and by direct injection into the body part affected, which is the clinical technique in common use, from out patient knee surgeries to diskectomies. The long needle is standard ER equipment for direct injection of epinephrine for cardiac arrest.

[60] See Maiden 2009; re cavitation inside skull Oehmichen et al. 2004, 2000; Karger 1995.

61 Komenda et al. 2013; Kaplan et al., 1998. If you're really cheap, the common and least expensive .38 cal. 158 gr. semi-wadcutter lead bullet in light target load might have similar effect.

62 See re therapeutic GKR: Matsunaga & Shuto 2014; Yeo & Yang 2012; Yen & Steiner 2011.

63 Henderson 2006, Appx. A. Currently Gallup's charts show over 60% favor the death penalty.

64 E.g., Re pattern of neg. prognosis, family consult & withhold/withdraw: Lesieur et al. 2015 (Leonetti Law France); Romain & Sprung 2014 (ICU care Israel); Masood et al. 2013 (ICU care UAE).

65 See Vellenga in Stassen, ed., 1998; Lukenbill 2009.

66 Blackstone, *Commentaries on the Common Law,* quoted in Granucci 1969 (p. 862); most states require a higher level of culpability for homicide to merit the death penalty. Evans 2012, Table 5.1.

67 *E.g.*, Dr. Michael Dixon MD in a 2012 case was accused of the murder of Dr. Joseph Sonnier MD in Lubbock, TX, allegedly motivated by jealousy over a woman; per var. Nov. 2015 news accounts the girlfriend testified against Dixon, the first case ended in a mistrial, and the case was being retried.

68 For examples: Mis-schedule surgery on parent's wishes so Down's child dies (Brock 1992); assisted suicide (Gostin 1993); withdrawing life support (Mueller 2009). Some of these actions are now legalized or de facto legal in several jurisdictions as discussed. See fn. 32-39 & accompanying text.

69 Dr. Harold Shipman of Britain is the most notorious MD. About 215 victims were identified per the Shipman Inquiry Board 2002, although he was convicted of only 15 deaths. Dr. Shipman used diamorphine (heroin), commonly used for palliative care for terminal illness in Britain, to kill his victims. In U.S.A., mivacurium chloride and pancuronium bromide are two of the sedatives that have been injected in serial patient homicides; pancuronium bromide (Pavulon) is used for lethal injections. The 'leading' U.S.A. medical killer is Charles Cullen, a night nurse, who killed an estimated 400 patients with a variety of drugs before his arrest; according to one author, he was fired by several hospitals 'under suspicion' but unreported, so was able to move from hospital to hospital. Graeber 2014.

70 Per L.A. Times, Dr. Hsiu-Ying 'Lisa' Tseng DO, was convicted in L.A., CA, U.S.A., in October 2015 of 2d Degree Murder for over-proscribing controlled substances to addicted patients. The annual report of doctors 'busted' for controlled substance offenses by the U.S. Drug Enforcement Agency is on line at: http://www.deadiversion.usdoj.gov/crim_admin_actions/doctors_criminal_cases.pdf .

Chapter 5:

The Bio-Medical Mechanics of

Death by Execution

All of the currently legal methods of execution have a common physiology of death by *acute ischemic anoxia* (AIA) which means complete stoppage of blood flow and oxygen supply to brain tissues, except the gas chamber which is based on anoxia alone. The effect, depending on how fast and complete the stoppage of blood flow is, is *apoptosis* (slow cell death) or *necrosis* (fast cell death) from 'global' cerebral infarcts. Fast here is relative; within a minute of oxygen deprivation massive die off of brain cells begins. [71] Apoptosis is the process of 'natural' cell death mediated by enzymes associated with *hypoxic* (partial or low blood flow) events, and necrosis can imply a chemical or traumatic (i.e., blunt object) injury to the brain cells as well as anoxia. [72] Only in the context of autopsies and post mortem diagnostics is distinguishing apoptotic from necrotic cell death necessary, so I will use AIA or anoxia here to include both forms of brain cell death in executions.

AIA (*acute ischemic anoxia*) and chemical anoxia are common to *all* forms of legal execution but the precise mechanism of getting that result differs. Anoxia is common to all forms of legal execution because they stop the flow of blood– by drug induced heart failure in lethal injection, constriction of blood supply by hanging, impact destruction of the heart muscle in firing squad, de-fibrillation and myocardial infarction of the heart by electric shock in the electric chair, and by chemical blockage of oxygen uptake in cyanide gas chamber executions. As soon as the heart stops pumping blood or the blood supply is constricted, oxygen deprivation causes a die off of nerve cells in the brain– that's why hypoxia damages the brain and anoxia kills.

There are variable "side effects" of the different methods of execution, but generally the cause of death is the same. Indeed, its the "side effects" of the method of execution that provide much of the motivation for opposition to the death penalty and the claim it is cruel or barbaric, etc.. This is a bit ironic since the U.S. Supreme Court's typical emphasis in death penalty cases is not how brutal it is, but how fair the process was in reaching a verdict of death, such as considerations of racial bias, access to evidence, witness or juror or evidence 'tampering' and so on. That is appropriate since done correctly all legal methods of execution will result in a rapid death, at least by yesteryear's standards. The fact executions aren't always done correctly and mistakes either prolong death or contribute to undesirable side effects, adds a lot of unfortunate 'gory details' and prompts most of the resultant, resilient, illogical emotional element in the controversy over the death penalty. [73]

I initially intended to discuss a 'cruelty scale' in this book for the various methods of legal execution and demonstrate a modern hanging is the most reliable at inducing a quick death with least inferred sensate awareness or death throes. I believe that to be the case, but I decided against the scale. Issues such as whether a sedated condemned is still conscious during a lethal injection and experiences a 'drowning feeling' during the paralysis phase, [74] or how much of the apparent body movement in the electric chair is experienced vs. insensate, or 'merely' involuntary muscle contractions from current flow, or at just what point brain death is reached in the gas chamber, is a mistake. That's because a focus on such 'visual clues' reverts to the same speculative and mistaken 'observations' of the crowd at public hangings that mistook the autonomic muscle-flexing of a brain dead corpse as 'death struggles' discussed in prior chapters. And where the observed effects are alleged to be "botched" executions, that focus on exceptions swallows the rule of efficient killing in the vast majority of executions by any method. Nor is there any reliable way to obtain an objective and scalable measure of cruelty since the term lacks precision and its impossible to know for sure post mortem what sensate experiences, if any, the deceased had once an execution began. Not even a modern autopsy supported by CT and MRI scans, laboratory tissue and blood chemistry tests, and similar technology on down to electron microscope scans of damaged tissue, will reveal what the pre-mortem subjective experiences of the corpse were with any certainty. [75]

Instead, the focus should be on efficiency in inducing anoxia for a given method of execution. AIA induced death is quick and relatively painless. That is, it is in the sense that 'painless' and 'quick' are the correlates of 'humane' (or at least more humane) where the opposite is 'cruel' (or 'barbaric' etc.), and prolonged. As I said in the Introduction, there is no truly painless death for a sensate organism. A state killing cannot transform into a 'pleasant' experience for the condemned. Some degree of significant discomfort is simply a practical reality that cannot be helped in judicial executions. For these reasons efficient does not imply pain free. It implies the method is effective and not prolonged. To put that in concrete terms, following are my 'takes' on the merits and demerits of current legal forms of execution.

The electric chair was a legal form of execution for a long time despite the cause of death being uncertain. I am persuaded most of the alleged suffering was imputed to a corpse because the great majority of executions in which 2000 volts was applied directly to the skull, resulted in a near instant death. The observed burning and shuddering and convulsive muscle contractions and 'frothing' and the like, were the result of the effects on the corpse of the current and resultant heat build up in the corpse, because the current was kept on 'just to be sure' the condemned was dead past the point of actual death. [76]

On the other hand, because the method of placing the electrodes on the skull and an ankle essentially mimics a lightening strike or high voltage electric arc accident that passes high voltage current through the body, autopsies and post mortem cause of death assessments were inconclusive because of the total body organ damage done. That made it difficult at best to allocate death to any one organ failure any more than it would be in a lightening strike death. Heart death is a common finding in high voltage accidental death and lightening strike post mortem assessments. That implies heart death and ischemic brain death may be the primary cause of death in an electrocution execution. [77] Whether any pain is experienced depends on the effect of 2000 volts on the neurotransmitters at the cellular level in the brain– my take is the nervous system is simply overwhelmed and consciousness 'as we know it' instantly lost. [78]

For these reasons I conclude an electrocution execution would not be 'cruel or unusual' method of execution *provided* its mechanism for inducing anoxia is efficient. It is unrealistic to expect, however, that the horrific effect on public imagination that old style electrocution execution conjures, can be overcome by assurances that's just a corpse jumping in the chair like the frog leg in high school biology. In that respect the electric chair (even if it is only made public by press coverage) resembles the *political spectacle executions* referred to above that were intended to intimidate the underclass, and that the 8th Amendment was intended to 'outlaw' in U.S.A.. [79] To draw an analogy from penology's past, even if it was a badly kept secret that the executioner garroted women executed for witchcraft or treason before burning at the stake, most people were horrified as the flames consumed human flesh. Similarly, 'jacking' the corpse with electricity is still horrific.

Getting back to the 21st Century, it is probable that an electrocution execution could be made tolerable only by eliminating as far as possible the spectacle caused by running current through the corpse. That is, by administering sufficient short-term voltage to cause instantaneous heart death, which in turn creates a blood stoppage to the brain and brain death. But then the current must be stopped. If the current is kept on it mutilates the corpse superficially by burning but also destroys internal organ tissue other than the heart, including the lungs and brain as the temperature of the corpse rises. The latter effect makes the objection electrocution 'cooks' the prisoner plausible and renders it an inefficient execution, if only because of the wasted power.

Definitely not advisable in my estimation, is the practice of jolting the prisoner for a few seconds & stopping to check for a heart beat and if she has a pulse, jolting her again That is an artifact of the imprecise 'whole body' head to ankle circuit created by the metal cap and ankle wire, when the condemned is strapped into the electric chair. That might have been state of the art in 1925; it is not today.

In this instance, ethical fastidiousness of an electrical engineer rather than a doctor may become problematic in upgrading 'old tech' electric chair electrocution. But the point is that a modern electrocution execution designed to induce AIA as efficiently as feasible is not 'cruel or unusual' punishment merely because it first kills the heart muscle to kill the brain. But that probably means dusty old "Sparky" might have to be scrapped in favor of 'fore and aft' sticky electrodes straddling the heart, or something of the kind, to focus the current flow to the heart instead of the overall body. But done that way it is likely the heart can be stopped essentially instantaneously and far less likely an electrocution execution will 'torture' the corpse.

The biggest draw back to the firing squad is the inconsistency of the aim of the shooters who reportedly often miss the little target placed over the heart of the condemned, with random hits to the body. Adapting the Twenty-Six Cent Solution and test barrel described in the last chapter to this situation might resolve the problem. If the firing mechanism were automated it would also relieve the police of the duty to pull the trigger, so to speak. The tried and true military .45 cartridge might be best here, to generate a larger wound channel in the torso. But the impact of a traditional lead bullet would reliably and instantly inflict fatal damage the heart muscle [80] with substantially less mutilation of the corpse than impact of multiple high velocity rifle bullets. [81] But you see the point that close-range discharge of the 'test' barrel targets the heart directly, stopping circulation and causing death.

In the case of lethal injection, it might be best to simplify the 'recipe' by substituting a large dose of methadone for the sedative and paralytic, increase the dosage of the chloride compound, and increase the interval of two injections to 5 minutes or more to give the opiate more time to work. Because AIA follows heart death efficiency equates to rapid heart death. Thus, increasing the chloride compound dosage (which induces cardiac arrest) targets AIA directly by generating a higher 'spike' in the blood serum concentration that induces heart failure in a lethal injection execution.

I have always assumed the real reason for the paralytic is to prevent thrashing and convulsions and the like. But a direct injection of an anesthetic into the heart (as suggested in the last chapter), instead of intravenous injection of the cloride, would stop the heart almost instantaneously and minimize any death throes since AIA would be even more rapid. Enough methadone would mitigate autonomic reflexive movement.

If the objective is efficiency in inducing AIA (which is 'better' to the extent there can be 'better' for the condemned) this approach tends to eliminate the need for a paralytic and eliminates the implication it is really palliative care for the public intended to avoid a 'spectacle' on the gurney. Like the Brampton's idea in the last chapter the methadone dose is likely to be far more popular on Death Row than a paralytic. But rapid onset AIA is the objective by whatever pharmaceuticals do the job best.

The gas chamber like the electric chair is problematic for me because of its inherent inefficiency in being based on a rising atmospheric concentration of a toxin (the parts-per-million ratio) within the gas chamber. It was sloppy in the beginning when few involved had any real idea what the physiological effects of the gas were, nor the proper ratios of a liquid acid to cyanide 'salt' added to generate the gas, and so on. It was later refined and, for a time at least, the California gas chamber at San Quintin Prison on San Francisco Bay was the state of the art for executions. But the rising plume of toxic gas that has to be breathed in and the time it takes for the cyanide to reach a sufficient concentration in the blood to be effective, all strikes me as inefficient and inherently slow in inducing anoxia.

As mentioned, the gas chamber does not involve AIA because there is no ischemia– just the opposite. The technique requires plenty of blood flow to work since it depends on cyanide in the blood blocking the uptake of oxygen by the brain tissues. It also starves the heart muscle for oxygen until it infarcts; if that happens before complete brain death an ischemia can be said to happen in a gas chamber execution. The secondary effects of death in the gas chamber of gasping, convulsions, 'frothing' at the mouth, urination and defecation are likely autonomic reactions analogous to the agonistic effects of the suicidal and erotic hangings already discussed.

If there is a method of execution that entails assurance of conscious discomfort it is probably the gas chamber. The condemned is not sedated because a normal to rapid pulse is indicated for uptake and distribution of the cyanide in the blood stream. I suppose that could be mitigated by giving thorazine first and then administering an 'upper' (caffeine would work) to raise the heart rate when the cyanide pellets are dropped into the acid cup, to try to speed the process. But the reality is the gas chamber is almost certainly the least efficient method of inducing anoxia, even if it is not 'cruel or unusual' in the legal sense.

I gave some thought to what would make this method efficient. One idea was to use a sort of helmet, like a diver's helmet, in lieu of the chamber. That would permit using concentrated pre-prepared gas from a tank like a diver's tank to increase the rate of uptake and cause a 'spike' in the serum concentration of cyanide in the blood to induce rapid anoxia. Rapid anoxia in this context of efficiency in inducing death could be said to be more humane. But I felt that was more likely to provide only middling improvement in an inherently inefficient method because the efficiency of the method still depends on the hard to control variables of rate of respiration and heart rate that tend to determine the rate of uptake of cyanide to the blood stream.

A 'new' idea that has been advanced is to substitute nitrogen or a noble gas for cyanide 'laced' air in the gas chamber, essentially drowning the condemned in a non-aqueous medium. That is so far only legal as an alternate in Oklahoma. I mention it because of its similarity to the cyanide gas method and because of yet another alternative.

I am sure its not the first time it has been suggested, but the likely very best 'humane upgrade' is to use ordinary carbon monoxide gas in the gas chamber. Notoriously, CO puts you to sleep before it induces death, referred to as "carbon monoxide intoxication" and "carbon monoxide poisoning" clinically. [82] CO toxicity is a result of the hyper affinity of hemoglobin for the CO molecule that 'locks out' O2 at the binding receptor, and prevents transport of O2 to the brain. [83] A clinical sign of carbon monoxide poisoning is bright cherry-red lips from the distinctive color of the resulting *carboxyhemoglobin* molecule. The net effect is myocardial hypoxia causing AIA and brain death. [84]

Because it is odorless, colorless and nonirritating, CO could be substituted for cyanide in existing gas chambers and released gradually until the condemned passes out. Because this is a passive process and CO can't be smelled or tasted it induces minimal physical discomfort compared to cyanide gas. It also eliminates the 'spectacle' of the condemned attempting to hold breath and the like, since the point of unconsciousness can't be anticipated. [85] Once unconscious, the CO concentration in the chamber could then be rapidly increased to a lethal level. [86]

This might be called the Devonian Pillow Solution, given the carbon rich atmospherics of that period and the fact it puts the condemned to sleep. Because it is not legal as a substitute gas in any state, I can't advance it here as a 'best' means of legal execution. But substituting CO gas for cyanide in the gas chamber would entail far and away less sensate experience than the current protocol for the gas chamber, the electric chair, firing squad, and much less even than the current lethal injection method of execution. By putting the sedation effect of CO on the same graduated scale as lethality from CO, the 'smooth slide' into oblivion of the Devonian Pillow Solution eliminates a separate pharmacological step of the lethal injection protocol than could be "botched" with too little or too late sedative effect. [87] And I doubt a prisoner would fake unconsciousness knowing that as soon as he or she did the CO gas would ramp up. Once a CO protocol is known, the great majority ought to walk in and sit for their fate knowing they won't "feel a thing" once they pass out in the chamber. [88]

The last issue in this chapter is the mental state of the prisoner on entering the area where the execution is to take place. Fear and anxiety are another matter that is unavoidable in a state killing, at least unless a method is used that "takes out" the condemned "unawares" he or she is being executed. I know of no jurisdiction that allows that to happen. An irony of the arguments against the death penalty is the claim life imprisonment causes prolonged mental stress and despair from confinement and thus endless punishment for life. That may or may not be true depending on the prisoner since some 'thrive' in a prison environment. But in my view, there can only be 'cruel and unusual' mental suffering associated with state killing if it is intentionally inflicted or a careless by-product of inefficient methodology. That makes the objective of efficient killing apply to mental as well as physical discomfort.

What is certain is that, depending on how well prepared for death the condemned is according to his or her beliefs, there will be some level of anxiety no matter what method of execution is deployed in a state killing. If the public policy of the jurisdiction permits the death penalty, then that is the unavoidable emotional concurrent to whatever sensate experience there is at the moment of death, that cannot be helped when the death penalty is lawfully imposed.

That said, leaving this world can be a matter of personal style. In the "last words" of the condemned, there have been many examples of the human condition: Grace and dignity (Lady Jane Grey who forgave the axe-man); heroics (Nathan Hale who declared, "I regret I have but one life to give"); steady nerves (Tom Horn who braided his own hanging rope); wistfulness (Johnny Green who said, "Yeah, I'd rather be fishing."); politics (John Spenkelink, who declared "Capital punishment– them without the capital gets the punishment."); or faith (Karla Tucker who calmly said, "I am going to be face to face with Jesus now."). You can never know for sure until the test of fortitude comes.

---

[71] Re ischemic "cascade" of fatal cellular NMDA excitotoxicity, calcium overload and oxidative stress: Caldelario-Jalil 2009; Rosenblum, W. 1997. Re DNA defragmentation: Dawson & Dawson 2004.

[72] Glucose sugar is the other component of blood that is essential to brain cells. Because the medical literature tends to focus on oxygen in brain death, I follow suit; however deprivation of glucose contributes to rapid death of brain cells and is a factor in ischemic events since it's blood born like O2.

[73] A knife is an essential kitchen tool until a 'motive' picks it up; an automobile is essential transportation until a 'blood alcohol' slips behind the wheel. In

the same way the term "botched" implies the reply executions overall are competent. The few mistakes are not a reason to ban the death penalty.

74 See re awareness during anesthesia: Bischoff et al. 2015; Hernandez-Meza et al. 2015; Errando, et al. 2008; Schwender et al. 1995.

75 See review of imaging techniques, Morgan et al. 2014; also Ferner 2008 (pharmacology); Colbourne et al. 1999 (electron microscope).

76 Brandon 1999, relating practices of Robert G. Elliot, long term electric executioner in New York and Massachusetts; Abbott 2006, p 94-95, quoting autopsy findings; Hillman 1993.

77 Re lightening strike: Sanford & Gamelli 2014 (cardiorespiratory arrest); Cooper 1995 (cardiac arrest).

78 Re lightening and high-voltage electrocution in emergency setting see: Edlich et al. 2005; Cooper 1995 (tinnitus, blindness, confusion, amnesia of survivors); Fontana Rosa 1993; Fish 1993.

79 I can imagine what sort of *danse macabre* Henry VIII and his executioners might have made of electricity, Henry having been a prolific *impresario* of public spectacle executions in his day.

80 Cause of death is usually attributed to hemorrhage secondary to a cardiac penetration wound; survival rate is 20% or less *after* reaching ER *if* sinus rhythm is present else 0%. See Degiannis et al, 2006 (109 case ER study); Lateef, et al., 2012 (review military lit.); Asencio, et al., 1998 (105 case ER study).

81 Wounds from high velocity non-expanding military rifle ammo can be less lethal than lower velocity expanding hand gun ammo. Santucci & Chang 2004; Padrta et al. 1997; also Maiden 2009.

82 Bleeker 2015; Thom Keim 1989.

83 Bleeker op cit; Prokop & Chichova 2007; Kao & Nañagas 2004; Raub & Benignus 2002.

84 The heart muscle is "most sensitive" to CO. Raub, et al. 2000. The technical term for insufficient oxygenation of the blood is *hypoxemia*. Pierson 2000.

85 The reason for installing CO sensors along side smoke detectors in the home is exactly because the gas is virtually undetectable by humans.

86 The perception it is painless is likely why the 'water hose taped to the exhaust pipe of running automobile' suicide is common or at least commonly attempted in U.S.A.; inept piping jobs and the 'leaky chamber' a suburban garage represents would not be factors in the controlled setting of a sealed prison gas chamber with graduated release using a pressure tank of pure CO.

87 Koniaris et al. 2005.

88 That will be seen as a drawback by many who not only advocate the death penalty but feel making it too easy misses the point in deterrence, vindication and closure. And no doubt there will on occasion be a Charles Campbell type that will put up resistance or act out in the chamber. But like Campbell they all meet their fate just the same when the justice system is working.

Chapter 6:

Instantaneous Ischemic Anoxia

by Constriction

If anoxia is common to all forms of legal execution as the cause of death and the relative merits of a given method depend at least in part on how efficient that method is in inducing anoxia, as discussed in the last chapter, then the most efficient method is hanging. Hanging causes an instantaneous ischemic anoxia by constriction of the carotid arteries and jugular veins (together with secondary arteries and veins) when the noose suddenly and tightly constricts around the neck at the end of the drop. As discussed in the first chapter, within a matter of seconds, unconsciousness occurs even in an 'amateur' suicidal hanging event with little or no drop. All of the sequelae discussed in Chapter 1 occur even more rapidly in a long drop execution conducted according to the British/U.S. Army protocol. Other than possibly a decapitation under the Guillotine, there is no faster or more complete ischemic effect, since among others, it is not dependent on killing the heart muscle as in a lethal injection, 'cooking' the heart and brain in the electric chair, or entail the gas chamber time lapse while the atmospheric cyanide gas is breathed in and begins to block oxygen uptake, wherein there is potential for sensate and emotional experience.

Instead, in a competent long drop hanging, anoxia begins instantly and the brain in effect sustains a series of widening strokes throughout the frontal and temporal lobes and the mid-brain, as the oxygen in the blood trapped in the skull is depleted, the blood 'puddles' in the arteries and veins as systolic pressure stops, and necrosis of neural tissues ('grey matter') begins *en masse*. The spondylolisthesis (complete vertebral dislocation) or subluxation (partial dislocation) of cervical verebra that damages the spinal cord, causes paralysis and accelerates the effect. As discussed below VAI (vertebral artery injury) and resulting lower brain edema is also a factor.

Because the effect is anoxia not hypoxia none of the brain cells escape because the strokes are not confined to a segment of the arterial or venous network, as happens in survivable strokes of the elderly. Instead the brain dies completely, but so fast the first symptom is unconsciousness within 15 seconds as discussed in Chapter 1.

Unconsciousness may also result from reflex cardiac arrest by direct compression of the enervated carotid sinus by the noose, which causes an almost instantaneous 'stutter' (*bradiarrhythmia*) of the heart with steep drop in blood pressure. This a well known condition referred to clinically as "neurally mediated reflex syncope" and vasovagus response. [89] But the effect is the same whether this syncope intervenes or not, that is, unconsciousness.

This 'beneficial' syncope effect has been inferred when the condemned is 'out cold' and limp at the end of the rope almost instantly. It has been suggested it can be induced if a double wrapped noose is used to help ensure compression of the carotid sinus. Others have attributed it to placement of the noose and micro-anatomy of the individual. Whether this syncope effect occurs or not, [90] the primary consequences to the condemned is brain death that occurs rapidly after the sudden and all-at-once constriction of the noose cuts off the blood supply to the head, combined with spinal injury from the mechanical shock force at the end of the drop. [91]

The very lowest portion of the human hind brain, the stem of the *medulla oblongata* extends through the *foramen magnum* where at approximately the level of the C2 vertebrae, the spinal cord begins. The medulla oblongata is a primitive and important part of the brain and its nerve centers have roles in controlling respiration, nervation, and blood flow. The medulla oblongata is served by two principal arteries, the *anterior spinal artery* and the *posterior inferior cerebellar artery* which are supplied by the vertebral arteries. The vertebral arteries are supplied by the *subclavian arteries,* that branch away from the lower *carotid arteries* which in turn, divide at or near the *carotid sinus* to form the *internal* and *external carotid arteries* (at about the level of the point of the jaw) bilaterally in the human neck.

Why this matters to a discussion of execution by hanging, is the vertebral arteries are protected by passing through the *foramen* of the *transverse process* of the first six cervical vertebrae, which are little loops of bone on the sides of the vertebra that keep the artery and associated veins and nerves in place along the side of the cervical column when the neck bends and rotates. The vertebral arteries branch off bilaterally from the subclavian arteries to enter the foramina at the C6 level, but emerge from the C1 foramen over the top of its upper surface in a notch called the *sulcus*, enter the *dura mater* and join to become the *basilar artery* [92] which is a major source of blood supply to the medulla oblongata.

This impacts constriction in a hanging because the vertebral arteries are both protected and supplied from a source below the main carotid arteries which align with the cervical spine but are outside the boney structures. Keeping it simple, complete or near complete constriction of blood flow via the much bigger carotid arteries, which are the main source of blood supply to the entire brain, is relatively easy by ligature (or grasping hands in a strangulation, keeping the penal purpose of this work in mind). Because the vertebral arteries are deeper under the other tissues of the neck, such as the large sternocleidomastoid and other muscles, and partially protected by bone, even a very tight constriction in a non-judicial hanging above C5-C6 (or potentially even in judicial hanging) may result in only partial constriction of the vertebral arteries.

There are internal and external jugular veins, the internal running along the carotid arteries and the external being alongside the prominent sternocleidomastoid muscle. It is the 'exposed' or vulnerable position of the external jugular to injury that gives rise to the expression 'go for the jugular.' However, because the major veins are no deeper than the carotid arteries, they become compressed by the ligature in a hanging, blocking the brain return blood flow. To put the foregoing into bio-mechanical terms, it has been reported that the force needed to compress the jugular is 2kg, carotid artery 5 kg, but to compress the vertebral artery is 20 kg. [93]

All of the foregoing bears on the physiology of anoxia in a hanging death. The vertebral arteries are the best protected in the neck structure and supply essential heart and breathing neurons in the 'primitive' medulla oblongata of the lower brain stem, an obvious evolutionary artifact. [94] But the higher brain is supplied by the carotid arteries and those are the most compromised by constriction of the ligature in a hanging. The rapid onset of unconsciousness is a direct consequence of the loss of blood supply to the cerebral cortex and onset of necrotic cell death. The more complete the constriction the more rapid and complete the level of necrosis of nerve tissues. This accounts for the rapid loss of consciousness in both short drop accidental & self-homicide and long drop judicial hanging discussed in detail above.

But one argument that has been advanced against hanging as a method of execution is that effective constriction of the jugular veins results in cerebral hemorrhage (or 'pooling' of blood inside the skull), which puts pressure on the brain causing a so-called "thunderclap headache." *Subarachnoid hemorrhage* (SAH) is a common emergent crisis from a rupture of a swelling (*aneurysm*) in a brain blood vessel, and often fatal. [95]

This idea of blood pumping in that can't get out of the skull causing 'massive' pain, is an aspect of anti-death penalty arguments that death is protracted, similar to arguments based on the autonomic kicks and gasps of the agonal sequence during suspension described in Chapter 1, during a hanging. This argument has some plausibility despite the seeming counter intuition that blocking veins and arteries at the same time should equalize. But when I first read the autopsies for the Dodd and Campbell judicial hangings in Washington state, I was struck by the finding of subarachnoid hemorrhage (SAH) in both decedents, despite the disparate cervical trauma autopsy findings in 1994. [96] That seemed to potentially corroborate the painful hemorrhage argument against judicial hanging.

But on further research it turns out that VAI has been well associated with emergent cervical trauma and consequent SAH and other brain edema. [97] And especially over the last five to seven years vertebral artery injuries have emerged as an important area for emergency surgery because of its occult symptoms or delayed symptoms, that can result in death despite good surgery to stabilize a cervical spine fracture. [98] In part the diagnosis has been vastly aided by sonography, tomography and magnetic resonance and similar technology that allows the ER surgeons to 'see' more deeply and see past 'expected' neurological trauma, guided by symptoms that are atypical for cervical injury but typical of ischemic injury to brain tissue. [99]

The gross cause is blunt force trauma to the vertebral artery complex– such as during auto accidents– but the ischemic mechanism can vary from a platelet or other 'debris' from the wound site being carried into the brain causing a stroke-like infarct on to damage to the artery itself causing a loss of or reduced blood flow. The diagnosis is complicated and the onset of symptoms can be delayed because if the injury is not bilateral, blood flow from the opposite artery compensates; but if the injury to the vertebral arteries is bilateral the outcome is likely to be fatal as a result of ischemic cerebral infarct of the tissues served by these blood vessels. [100]

The reason for this mini-review of the clinical literature relating to VAI is the association with cervical trauma and common cerebral edemas translates 'well' to the injuries reported for a long drop judicial hanging, including the SAH reported for the Washington state executions described by Wallace et al. in 1994. For example in both cases the vertebral arteries sustained trauma and in one case the SAH was in the lower skull, and in the other in the higher spinal column. [101] Indeed the association with motor vehicle accidents and blunt force trauma etiology of cervical fracture and dislocation for VAI makes the translation even stronger. That leads me to conclude the SAH observed on autopsy after cervical hanging executions follows on the initial shock and unconsciousness.

On the other hand, the lingering vital signs such a pulse or respiratory contractions, suggest not all brain tissue is killed outright. I am suggesting as a 'forensic hypothesis' that limited blood flow to the (primitive) medulla oblongata via the vertebral arteries keeps the neurons of the nerve centers of the medulla oblongata alive after death of the cerebral cortex in those cases where the injury to the vertebral arteries is unilateral or otherwise results in a reduction in blood flow but not a complete obstruction. That would account for ongoing neurological response from the lower brain keeping a semblance of heart and respiratory function going for the reported three or four minutes, sustained by a partial blood supply to the 'primitive' medulla oblongata.

It also occurred to me that the likely indicia this occurs would be evidence of apoptosis of the indicated nerve tissues rather than necrosis. The bio-chemical markers for apoptosis and its precursors are known [102] so that micro-autopsy of the target tissues, secondary to dissection of the vertebral arteries and assessment of injury, ought to reveal whether the tissues survived for long. Evidence of tissue death from apoptosis of the neurons in the *solitary neucleus* and 'centers' (vasomotor, cardiac and respiratory) of the medulla oblongata might tend to support the hypothesis 'trickle' circulation from the protected vertebral arteries accounts for persistent vital signs after rapid death of other (larger) parts of the brain from arterio/venous constriction ischemia in judicial hanging.

What of the 'thunderclap headache' (TCH) associated (but not exclusively) with SAH as a diagnostic symptom in the emergency and clinical setting? It is unclear if the cause is pressure, toxicity or something else, and the fact it is associated with other conditions indicates TCH is not a universal symptom of SAH with its various causes. [103] On the other hand, TCH is commonly associated with VAI dignostically. [104] But possible TCH supports an inference (and consequent 'anti' argument) that the condemned who sustains SAH and/or VAI may suffer 'cruel' pain during a judicial hanging.

However, I can offer the better 'educated guess' the condemned is unlikely to experience any sensation or consciousness for more than a very few seconds after the drop. The trauma to the spine and constriction of the carotid arteries and jugular veins, with rapid AIA and observed rapid loss of consciousness fits the profile of "sudden brain death" too well. [105]

In an article commonly cited by death penalty opponents by Harry Hillman (Perception 1993), Hillman discusses potential suffering of various methods of death penalty. For hanging, he acknowledges loss of sensation below the neck but posits pain via the trigimenal neural pathway (i.e, facial). Although the trigimenal nerves do emerge from the mid-brain well above C1-C2, the midbrain is served by the carotid arteries and their branches. Necrosis of the midbrain would thus be as rapid and complete as the rest of the brain resulting from constriction-ischemia, especially in a long drop hanging, along with the neurons of the trigimenal complex. And that is aside from the rapid onset of unconsciousness discussed above that would mitigate any such secondary pain.

Another working hypothesis for which I found very little medical information in context of hanging, is *contra coup* injury to explain SAH. SAH is a common result of contra coup injury which is essentially a traumatic side to side 'slap' of the brain tissue against the inside of the skull. It is found in various events in which the head strikes a hard surface, such as on being ejected from a moving vehicle, falling from a scaffold and striking the frame, and *very* common in skateboarding accidents. [106] It poses a Newtonian physics problem of the 'delta-v' forces calculated in accident reconstruction, that is, because the moving head and body suddenly halt but the brain's momentum causes the soft nerve tissues to impact the inside of the skull. Massive edema can be the result as well as direct impact injury to the tissues.

Since contra coup is a form of acceleration/deceleration injury it seemed to me that the sudden jolting stoppage of the body at the end of the long drop hanging might cause a form of contra coup injury to account for the SAH observed on autopsy after judicial hanging. But I found no published studies discussing this in an on-line search.

One last and interesting phenomenon is the hypoxic 'high' or intoxication reported to be common as a choking game among adolescents [107] and common in autoerotic asphyxia. [108] There are also numerous accounts of people who were intentionally or accidentally hanged, partially drowned, or sustained cardiac arrest or other emergent situation involving ischemic hypoxia, and lived to report an 'out of body' experience while comatose. The one thing conspicuously absent from reports of such experiences are reports of sensations of excruciating pain. Accounts of ecstatic ascents toward a white light, and so on, are the opposite. [109]

Whatever the induced 'thrill-sensations' of hypoxia are, the effects of hypoxia act on the nerve tissues directly, and the effects of a 'brain bleed' are indirect and require time to become symptomatic. It is thus inferred that the mental experiences of hypoxia are far more likely to be sensed before unconsciousness develops in a space of a minute or less, and consist of whatever neuro-excitation there is secondary to and symptomatic of direct neuropathology in hypoxia or anoxia. [110] Thus what is last felt could be sensations of the hypoxic 'high.'

I am reminded of speculations about consciousness after decapitation under the Guillotine, which resulted in some macabre experiments in which a prisoner was persuaded to 'blink' in response to questions posed to the 'head' after decapitation. Why the 'head' was asked to blink instead of smile or wiggle its ears, or whatever, I am not sure. Someone once offered as proof, that one is awake and aware holding your breath 3 minutes without oxygen, so why not the 'head' for a few moments at least? The difference is circulation of blood continues holding your breath and you are not suffering the shock of severing the spinal cord. Life of the 'head' in decapitation is not conscious even if there is a short survival of brain tissue before necrosis of the mass of brain tissues. If there is any sensation it might be a fleeting hypoxic high. But I bring decapitation and interrogating 'heads' up here because of the tendency for anti-death penalty advocates to assert horrific sensate experience *in extremis* that simply cannot be known for certain. In discussing sensation at all, I have only attempted to bring fact analysis to the discussion in some degree, to 'bust' the death penalty myths based on interpreting the muscle reflexes of someone already brain dead, if not already a corpse, to be agonized death 'throes.'

Whether any of the foregoing hypothesizing turns out to be bright or just 'brainstorming' the practical reality ought to be clear. Judicial hanging results in complete unconsciousness in 15 seconds or less, with rapid brain death by necrosis of the mass of cerebral tissues within about 100 seconds, followed by cardiac arrest within 6 minutes or less. The loss of consciousness within seconds at the end of the drop as a result of cervical injury and global ischemia means any sensate experience is of very short duration.

As a result hanging is an efficient means of state killing, much faster with less inferred sensory experience even than the 20 minutes or more of the lethal injection protocol. Modern judicial execution conforming to the British/U.S. Army protocol is therefore, despite its reputation as archaic, far more 'humane' than the gas chamber, electric chair, or lethal injection, and entails less risk of mutilation of the corpse than firing squad.

---

[89] Suárez-Peñaranda et al. 2013; Schrag et al. 2011 (cerebral hypoxia due carotid compression & reflex cardiac arrhythmia); Ogoh et al. 2004; Benditt et al. 1998. Interestingly, to induce the syncope response either carotid sinus massage or head tilt up or both are used in test subjects. Alboni et al. 1993; Kenny et al. 1993. It appears carotid sinus compression can itself cause death. Schrag et al. 2012. The symptomatic fainting has been characterized as *neurocardiogenic syncope*. Quan et al.1997.

[90] See re clinical data & reflex: Toorop et al. 2009; Alboni et al 1993; Kenny et al. 1993. See re judicial hanging Clément et al. 2010.

[91] A hangman's knot made with 13 turns of prestretched hemp rope is rigid and can 'slap' the head quite hard. The brass ring in a British method noose has been said to 'rap' the skull with force as well.

[92] Harsharvardhana & Dabke 2014, Fig. 1; Clark et al., in Klika, ed., 2011, Fig. 2.

[93] Arslan, et al., 2013; http://www.forensicpathologyonline.com/e-book/asphyxia/hanging .

[94] Reptiles for example have a brain structure resembling the 'hind brain' but lack the extensive 'add-on' neuro-anatomy of the human cerebrum that evolved in primates. Then again, reptiles are incapable of murder lacking that 'after-acquired' mass of neurons needed to form a *mens rea*.

[95] E.g., van Gijn & Rinkel 2001 (clinically SAH is a result of ruptured aneurysm "85% cases").

96   Wallace et al. 1994; see Hellier & Connolly 2009.

97   Uhrenholt et al. 2015; Lebl et al. 2013 (basilar skull fracture, occipitocervical dissociation, displacement transverse foramen [C6]); Fassett et al. 2008 (70% traumatic VAI have associated cervical fracture); Cothren et al. 2003 (fracture vertebra, fracture + subluxation, fracture *foramen transversum*); Leys et al.1997.

98   E.g., Donghwan et al. 2014; Kakao et al. 2014; Yoshihara et al. 2011.

99   Friedman et al. 1995; Fassett op cit. (still unclear which strategies best).

100 Donghwan et al. 2014; Yshihara et al. 2011; Wirbel et al. 1996.

101 Wallace et al. 1994, 264.

102 See re therapeutic applications: Fujikawa 2015 (DNA cleavage); Krijnen et al. 2002 (calcium & cytotoxic hypotheses); Martin et al. 1998 (NMDA); Rosenblum 1997.

103 Devenney et al. 2014; Ju & Schwedt 2010; Schwedt & Dodick 2006.

104 Schwedt 2015; Linn 2010; Matharu et al. 2007.

105 The hippocampus and deep folia of the cerebellum also sustain rapid necrosis by anoxia. Carrido & Bayarri in Tanasescu ed. 2012; Pierson 2000.

106 Tominga et al. 2015; Tominga et al. 2013. I am of two minds about making entertainment out of skateboard accidents that may amount to witnessing brain death or other permanent injury; if it works to inform youth ('seeing is believing') and that's a way to get them to "get it" about helmets then OK.

107 See. e.g., re "choking game" among adolescents: AlBuhairan et al. 2015; Barbería-Marcalain et al. 2010; CDC U.S. 2010, 2008.

108 See note 6 above. Re rate fatal erotic asphyxiation ligature/hanging: Savageau 2014, 2012; Savageau & Racette 2006; Janssen et al. 2005; Behrendt et al. 2002; Byard et al. 1990. Re association asphyxial eroticism and serial murder: Myers et al. 2008.

109 E.g., Hou et al. 2013; Bonilla 2011; French 2005; see also Anzellotti et al. 2011.

110 Neurotransmitter 'brainstorm' induced by anoxia in rats. Li, et al. 2015. Re human EEG coritical & hindbrain 'burst suppression' during coma: Japaridze, N., et al. 2015; Westover et al. 2015, Westover et al. 2013; Guéit 1999. Re using EEG for prognostics after anoxic-eschemia: Young, et al. 2005.

Chapter 7:

Updating the Long Drop Hanging Execution

The number one handicap in postulating improvements to a method of execution is the almost total inability to conduct trials. Unless a prisoner consented, an attempt to innovate a new technique would almost certainly add to the post-conviction cost of execution by appeals claiming the prisoner was being 'tortured' with experimental cruelties in U.S.A.. As in pharmacology, animal surrogates are possible and it turns out rabbits offer a surrogate because of a suitable cervical arterial system. [111] But as with drug trials some form of beta testing generally precedes approval. For that reason the Edwardian technique on which the U.S. Army protocol is based likely would have to be retained and innovation limited to the equipment.

Certain areas of improvement are simple. The rope for example. Hemp was the fiber of choice for rope for centuries because it was strong and relatively durable, especially favored during the "age of sail." But today there are very excellent synthetic ropes and some, like the ubiquitous synthetic 'static line' well known to rock climbers, tree trimmers, and first responders alike, offers an easy sliding, no-stretch alternative. The amount of stretch at the end of the drop was a persistent problem for the hangmen of old in calculating the drop in a judicial hanging. Use of modern rope would tend to eliminate that problem, albeit some minor adjustment to the drop table might be in order. Although in theory the table assumes a hemp rope has been prestretched, hemp is 'live' in the sense of the twined fibers constricting themselves under load and then releasing slightly. That is a miniscule issue with modern static line.

In American practice the thirteen turn hangman's knot has been traditional, an evolution from the Gallow's Knot, which it resembles. However the 3-4 turn Gallow's Knot is associated with strangulation hanging, as it was in use far earlier than the 13 turn hangman's knot. A supposed advantage of the 13 turn knot is that the friction of the extra turns hold it in place, and it facilitates cervical fracture. Mechanically, at about 10" in length tied with 3/4" hemp rope, the hangman's knot could tend to force the head to the side in subaural position, or force the head back in submental position.

The tradition of using 13 turns is actually a superstition of sorts. Assuming good quality rope, the hangman's knot is strong enough at the 3-4 turns of the older Gallows Knot to be used for hanging. The Army protocol is actually seven turns per the 1947 knot illustration. (See Appx. A) The reason for adding turns of rope in the modern era would be to adjust the alleged lever effect on the side of the head, assuming the traditional subaural knot placement is used. And some research would be needed toward compiling a separate table for tying the knot so that the top three turns lay medially against the temporal bone, likely adjusted to a simple measurement of the condemned's head, to obtain the benefit of any leverage.

However, the old Commonwealth method uses Marwood's roved brass ring to form the noose, not a knot. And the English in past and other nations in present reliably obtain cervical fracture hangings using the Commonwealth noose. That tends to imply the 13 turns are more a tradition-superstition than critical to an efficient killing by hanging. I discount any knot-lever effect and would tie a 7 turn hangman's knot put in subaural position.

Where the 13 turns (or possibly more or less by anatomic measurement) could have a more practical role, is in the submental placement of the knot. The tendency of the strand of the Commonweath noose was to slide off the point of the chin and along the jaw to the subaural position. That I suspect is why Marwood, although he clearly knew about the Irish submental method, possibly after a trial or two, simply placed the knot in the subaural position to begin with. A 13 turn knot on the other hand might tend to stay in place for a submental hanging since it is far 'stiffer' than the single strand of the brass ring noose. Some work with a crash dummy or similar surrogate to get appropriate length of knot (i.e., # of turns) to obtain a knot that stays in position for the submental execution, might be in order. Another possibility (in the Marwood tradition) would be use of a leather skull cap and chin cup held in place with straps, that would hold the jaw closed (to prevent tongue biting), and firm up submental placement of the knot with a 'sticky' adhesive (or possibly 'hook and loop' binding) on the outer surface of the chin cup, holding the knot in place but weak enough to break free easily on the drop. [112]

As discussed above the advantage of the submental position is that it reliably transfers all or almost all of the energy generated by the drop, in levering the head back onto the neck, onto the base of the occiput, atlas and axis (C1, C2), causing fractures with direct trauma to the stem of the medulla oblongata, and a spondylolisthesis that severs the spinal cord at the top of the spinal column. That would be the most efficient result for judicial hanging since death would be essentially instantaneous, even if reflexive autonomic movements of the corpse might follow, as discussed in greater detail above.

That said, the more common subaural position very reliably induces unconsciousness seconds after the drop with following sudden brain death by acute ischemic anoxia, with associated cervical trauma. The latter may include dislocation (subluxation) and fracture, and can include partial or complete spondylolisthesis, depending on the individual. The inconsistency shown by past reports of contemporaneous or anthropological osteopathic autopsies is known but not known why.

But the "Hangman's Fracture" is not consistent in clinical emergency setting either. I conclude the likely reason in judicial hanging is related to individual anatomy of neck musculature ('pencil neck' vs. 'no neck'), minor variables in exact knot position, tension of knot, and the 'life' in a hemp rope depending on how well and how recently it was stretched, all variables hard to account for retrospectively. [113] What is well known by modern forensic autopsy using tomographic, radiographic, pharmochemical and micro-dissection techniques, is that a competent judicial hanging causes certain and rapid death in either subaural or submental position, with cervical trauma in a competent Edwardian, that is, calculated drop hanging.

The breadth of the rope needs to be considered along with length of drop, since hard, thin ligatures may be more likely to result in decapitation than a larger diameter rope or cord. [114] A 3/4" 'manila' rope of the type Marwood used and as used today in some countries, has a working load of about 700 lb., obviously adequate in Marwood's day. But stature has increased in the modern era and so have weights. 6'4" and 250 lbs. would not be uncommon in the prison system.

A 3/4" rope is equivalent to a 19mm modern rescue line. Because of the lack of stretch in modern kernmantle static line and its great strength by comparison to hemp rope (hemp climbing rope has been obsolete since 1950), it would be an improvement. An 11 mm rope would have ample strength. But it would be narrow and thus have a potential for cutting in compression on the neck; at 19mm the same rope might be a bit 'stiff' by comparison to hemp, especially tied to 13 turns of the knot.

I would likely go instead with what is known as an arborist's 'bull rope' (double braided polyester type) of the traditional 3/4" diameter, a material that is designed to bear repeated loads, holds knots, is highly abrasion resistant, slick without being slippery, and has enormous strength (in the 2000 lb. working load range @ 8/1 ratio), far more than needed for hanging even a 300 lb. prisoner, in 3/4" size. Arborist rope is less expensive and widely available. Bright colors are the norm, but black, brown or dark blue can be found for prison work. The chief advantage in the modern rope is that the almost complete lack of stretch allows a very precise calculation of the rope length, or actual or 'true' drop, and thus energy transfer, based on the prisoner's height and weight. That makes for a more precise computation to obtain 1260 foot pounds of pressure (per the Washington State protocol), or to simply match the Army Drop Table.

The so-called 'collapse board' that was intended for a prisoner who was literally 'faint at heart' and passed out or 'goes limp' when approaching or mounting the gallows, presents an interesting potential. Even a prisoner well-strapped at ankle and waist Marwood style is a flexible weight with potential to bend or sway out of 'true' on the drop, or even put up a struggle. For that reason routine use of an 'improved' collapse board might be in order since the drop would be straighter and the transfer of force to the cervical spine more direct and efficient than if the drop ends with the body and thus the neck at an angle. [115]

The ordinary board made to the U.S. Army specification is a 1x6" plank with straps attached, 27" length, or just enough to bind the legs together so the prisoner (with arms strapped to the body with a Marwood style belt), can be propped up to complete the drop. (See Appx. A; note 27" is a bit short for many today.) To improve this, I would devise something like the lightweight synthetic back board used for emergency work (and familiar to athletic trainers), although in that application it is often intended to stabilize the cervical spine. In shape it would resemble a silhouette target, but expanded to 15" in width at the hips, 10" above, 6" as typical below, shallowly molded to approximate the contours of the human body, and with the tapered end intended to fit between the shoulder blades.(These dimensions are approximate and preparation of three S-M-L boards likely necessary, but retaining the calf-to-scapula parameter.) The edges would be slotted like an ambulance carry board to hold the straps and bind the prisoner upright in the 'attention' posture to meet his or her fate with the spine vertical.

The disadvantage of the traditional collapse board is the prisoner can still bend or twist or otherwise resist and thus fall at an angle and out of 'true' diminishing the effect of a calculated drop. As pointed out above, the inconsistency of fracture in subaural knot position is likely due in part to variation in the constriction and angle of fall, affecting the distribution of force around the ligature. That would be minimized if a longer, back and leg board were deployed together with the more precise calculation of fall a 'no stretch' type of modern rope permits.

The closer to vertical the prisoner falls the more directly the intended force is imparted to the cervical vertebra on the drop. The cumulative effect of no stretch and a modified collapse board would thus amplify and make the constriction pressure more uniform while reducing variation in the cervical trauma imparted by the shock force at the end of the drop. Again, in the sense that efficiency in killing is more 'humane' and less 'cruel' by shortening 'time-to-extremis' to the most practical minimum in carrying out a lawful sentence of death, such an improvement is to the advantage of both society and the condemned.

The Army manual clearly specifies the knot is to be placed behind the left ear. However there is evidence subaural originally meant anterior of the ear next to the point of the jaw in Marwood's day. Given the potential for the knot to slip toward the back of the neck, I would place it anterior to avoid that issue and gain partial submental 'leverage' toward inducing cervical trauma.

My final takes on what to change or not, are these:

1. Leave the traditional U.S. style hangman's knot in use since it is reliable;

2. Leave the 13 turns to the movies; a 7 turn knot is adequate in subaural position;

3. Leave the hemp rope to history; modern synthetic kernmantle static line (as used in rescue work [116]) or arborist's 'bull rope' is an improvement that by lack of stretch allows a more precise calculation of the force to be generated during the drop to induce fracture;

4. The traditional 3/4" breadth has been shown to work well and not cut into the neck if the drop is properly computed; a

modern 13 mm static line or arborist "bull rope" of 3/4" will have about 4x the needed load bearing and shock resistance capacity for an 300 lb. prisoner;

5. Because it aids in keeping the drop straight an improved collapse board to be used routinely;

6. The U.S. Army design for the scaffold and gallows needs no elaboration, other than possibly re-dimensioning the overall size of the platform and the size and weight bearing capacity of the trap door, to accommodate modern body height and weight ranges in an era when over 6' and 300 lbs. are common (unlike in Sgt. Woods' day when the average G.I. was 160 lbs. and 5' 8' or so). That may call for more working area; but given Woods's troubles at Nuremberg with the trap door, I would devise a ball-bearing hinge attached to the underside of the scaffold deck, to swing the trap door down and away 110 degrees and lock into place out of the way of the falling prisoner;

7. I'd keep the black paint and canvas curtains, but would favor stainless steel metalwork to iron, and use ordinary kiln dried Douglas fir lumber, as its strong, durable and workable; if I had the budget I'd use oak for the crossbeam of the gallows as an extra measure of strength and a nod to the common law; otherwise I would use a glulam roofing beam for its rigidity vs. lumber, and secure the rope as shown in the U.S. Army manual to a 7/8" eye bolt (an upgrade from 3/4" in U.S. Army manual bearing in mind size range of modern physique) through the beam and fix the length at the noose, rather than use a Marwood style chain and adjustable shackle fixed at the beam. [117]

THE END

---

[111] See Boghossian et al. 2010; Hirano et al. 1993; and see Clément, R., et al., 2010.

[112] If but only if the ideas expressed herein are used by a lawful, non-terrorist government entity for a penal purpose, the author disclaims any rights therein.

[113] See Clément et al. 2011.

[114] The most important factor is weight and length of drop; 12-13000 Newtons can produce a decapitation in accidental/suicidal hangings. Tóro et al. 2008; Rothschild & Snyder 1999; Rabl et al. 1995; Pankratz et al. 1986. Re forensic clues: Tsokos et al. 2004.

[115] See notes 5, 24 above.

[116] Rock climber's dynamic line is designed to stretch and is counter-indicated.

[117] Wood is indicated as metal invites lightening; if the scaffold and gallows' beam is to be permanent, a departure from the U. S. Army specifications might be to add one *finial* improvement.

APPENDIX A

Drop Table & U. S. Army 1947 protocol– excerpted from Pamphlet 27-4

p.8

SECTION III
EXECUTION BY HANGING

Officer Charged with Execution
The officer charged with the execution will command the escort and make the necessary arrangements for the conduct of the execution.   He will-.

a. Instruct components of the escort in their duties.
b. Arrange for the receipt of the prisoner by the prisoner guard.
c. Arrange for a chaplain to accompany the prisoner.
d. Arrange for the presence of a medical officer at the scene of the execution.
e. Provide a proper gallows.
f . Provide a black hood to cover the head of the prisoner.
g. Provide a collapse board for use if necessary.
h. Cause the prisoner's arms to be secured before or immediately upon his receipt by the prisoner guard. The arms may be secured either behind the back or in front, fastened to the belt (fig. 1).
i. Arrange for a burial party as prescribed in paragraph 13k.
j. Determine the proper amount of drop of the prisoner through the trap door. A standard drop chart for normal men of given weights is given below. Variation of the drop because of physical condition may be necessary. A

medical officer should be consulted to determine whether any factors, such as age, health, or muscular condition will affect the amount of drop necessary for a proper execution.

120 lbs or less	8' 1"	170 lbs	6' 0"
125 lbs	7' 10"	175 lbs	5' 11"
130 lbs	7' 7"	180 lbs	5' 9"
135 lbs	7' 4"	185 lbs	5' 7"
140 lbs	7' 1"	190 lbs	5' 6"
145 lbs	6' 9"	195 lbs	5' 5"
150 lbs	6' 7"	200 lbs	5' 4"
155 lbs	6' 6"	205 lbs	5' 2"
160 lbs	6' 4"	210 lbs	5' 1"
165 lbs	6' 2"	220 lbs and over	5' 0"

k. Rehearse the execution within 24 hours prior to the scheduled time for the execution. · A sandbag or similar object approximating the prisoner's weight may be used to insure proper functioning of the gallows, trap door, and hangman's noose.

Executioner
An official experienced executioner will be appointed. If one is not available to the command, a prof essional civilian executioner may be obtained and appointed ; payment at the local rate, but not to exceed one hundred dollars ($100.00) per execution, may be authorized and paid from Contingencies of the Army, Project 416.In the event a professional executioner is not available, a suitable emotionally stable member of the command will be selected andappointed executioner.

. . .
[p. 10]

Execution

a. If troops are present, the officer charged with the execution will face the prisoner and read aloud to him the charge, finding, sentence and orders.   He will then   notif y the chaplain and the, prisoner that a brief time will be allowed the prisoner for any last statement. Af ter a reasonable time he will have the execu- tioner place the hood over the prisoner's head and bind his ankles. The executioner will then adjust the noose around the prisoner's neck and remain beside the prisoner. The sergeant of the pris- oner guard or other individual designated _by the officer charged with the execution will then place himself in position at the trigger and, upon a signal from said officer, will spring the trap. The medical officer will then examine the body for time of death nd report to the officer charged with the execution.

b. Upon the pronouncement of the death of the prisoner, the escort, with the band playing a lively air, will return to the parade ground and be dismissed.

c. The witnessing troops will move to their respective areas where they will be dismissed.

d. The officer charged with the execution will direct the burial party in the disposal of the body as prescribed by the commanding officer.

. . .

SECTION VII EQUIPMENT

Hood

The hood will be black, the outer surface of rough materials, split at the open end so that it will come well down on the prisoner's chest and back.

Collapse Board and Binding Strap

a. A collapse board will be provided for use in case of the collapse of the prisoner. (See fig.5.)

Rope

The rope will be of manila- hemp, at least 3/4 inch and not more than 1 1/4 inches in diameter and approximately 30 feet in length. The rope will be boiled and then stretched while drying to eliminate any spring, stiffness, or tendency to coil. The hangman's knot (figure 7) will be used in the preparation of the noose. That portion of the noose which slides through the knot will be treated with wax, soap, or grease to insure a smooth sliding action through the knot. The noose will be placed snugly around the prisoner's neck in such a manner that the hangman's knot is directly behind his left ear.

Straps

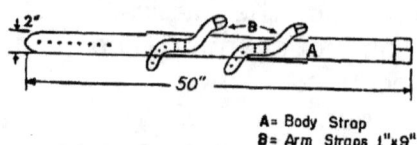

A= Body Strap
B= Arm Straps 1"x9"

Figure 1. Binding strap.

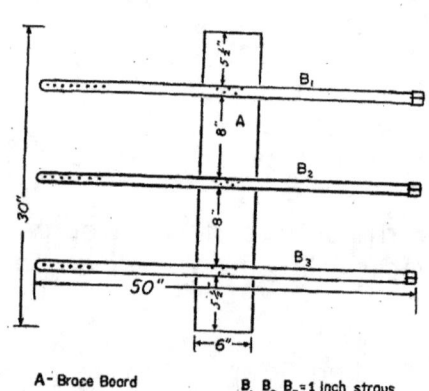

A - Brace Board   B₁ B₂ B₃ = 1 inch straps

Figure 5. Collapse board.

Knot

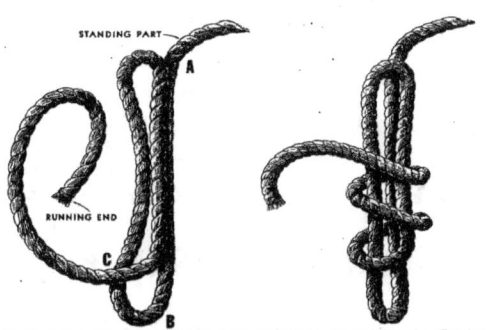

Length of loops: from A to B should be approximately 18 inches, and from C to Running End should be approximately 35 inches to 108 inches depending upon diameter of the rope. Wrap Running End around for six turns. No extra rope should remain.

Figure 7 ① and ②. Hangman's knot.

Tighten loops by pulling at Running End. Lock loops and form knot by pulling down at point D. Slide knot up or down on Standing Part to adjust size of loop.

Figure 7 ③ and ④.

☆U. S. GOVERNMENT PRINTING OFFICE: 1947—J. 751637—105

APPENDIX B:

BRITISH HOME OFFICE c. 1959 text:

"Note:- Attention is drawn to paragraph No. 12, which has been further revised."

Confidential

(By order of the Secretary of State, this document is to be treated as most strictly confidential, but the responsible Works Officer should be given the opportunity to study its contents. In any case when a copy is supplied to a Sheriff he is requested to return it to the Prison Governor from whom he received it.)

MEMORANDUM OF INSTRUCTIONS FOR CARRYING OUT AN EXECUTION

2. The trap doors shall be stained a dark colour and their outer edges shall be defined by a white line three inches broad painted round the edge of the pit outside the traps.

3. (a) A week before an execution the apparatus for the execution shall be tested in the following manner under the supervision of the Works Officer, the Governor being present:

The working of the scaffold will first be tested without any weight. Then a bag of dry sand of the same weight as the culprit will be attached to the rope and so adjusted as to allow the bag a drop equal to, or rather more than, that which the culprit should receive, so that the rope may be stretched with a force of not more than 1,000 foot-pounds. See Table of Drops. The working of the apparatus under these conditions will then be tested. The bag must be of the approved pattern, with a thick and well- padded neck, so as to prevent any injury to the rope and leather. Towelling will be supplied for padding the neck of the bag under the noose. As the gutta percha round the noose end of the execution ropes hardens in cold weather, care should be taken to have it warmed and manipulated immediately before the bag is tested.

(b) On the day before the execution the apparatus shall be tested again as above, the Governor, the Works Officer and the executioner being present. For the purpose of this test a note of the height and weight of the culprit should be obtained from the Medical Officer and handed to the executioner.

4. After the completion of each test the scaffold and all the appliances will be locked up, and the key kept by the Governor or other responsible officer; but the bag of sand should remain suspended all the night preceding the execution, so as to take the stretch out of the rope.

5. The executioner and any persons appointed to assist in the operation should make themselves thoroughly acquainted with the working of the apparatus.

6. In order to prevent accidents during the preliminary tests and procedure the lever will be fixed by a safety-pin, and the Works or other Prison Officer charged with the care of the apparatus prior to the execution will be responsible for seeing that the pin is properly in position both before and after the tests. The responsibility for withdrawing the pin at the execution will rest on the executioner.

7. Death by hanging ought to result from dislocation of the neck. The length of the drop will be determined in accordance with the attached Table of Drops.

8. The required length of drop is regulated as follows:

a. At the end of the rope which forms the noose the executioner should see that 13 inches from the centre of the ring are marked off by twine wrapped round the covering; this is to be a fixed quantity, which, with the stretching of this portion of the rope, and the lengthening of the neck and body of the culprit, will represent the average depth of the head andcircumference of the neck after constriction.

b. While the bag of sand is still suspended, the executioner will measure off from the painted line[1] on the rope the required length of drop, and will make a chalk mark on the rope at the end of this length. A piece of copper wire fastened to the chain will now be stretched down the rope till it reaches the chalk mark, and will be cut off there so that the cut end of the copper wire shall terminate at the upper end of the measured length of drop. The bag of sand will[2]

The chain will now be so adjusted at the bracket that the lower end of the copper wire shall reach to the same level from the floor of the scaffold as the height of the prisoner. The known height of the prisoner can be readily measured on the scaffold by a graduated rule of six foot six inches long. When the chain has been raised to the proper height the cotter must be securely fixed through the bracket and chain. The executioner will now make a chalk mark on the floor of the scaffold, in a plumb line with the chain, where the prisoner should stand.

c. These details will be attended to as soon as possible after 6 a.m. on the day of the execution so as to allow the rope time to regain a portion of its elasticity before the execution, and if possible, the gutta percha on the rope should again be warmed.

9. The copper wire will now be detached, and after allowing sufficient amount of rope for the easy adjustment of the noose, the slack of the rope should be fastened to the chain above the level of the head of the culprit with a pack-thread. The pack-thread should be just strong enough to support the rope without breaking.
10. When all the preparations are completed the scaffold should remain in charge of a responsible officer until the time fixed for the execution.

At the time fixed for the execution, the executioner will go to the pinioning room, which should be as close as practicable to the scaffold, and there apply the apparatus. When the culprit is pinioned and his neck is bared he will be at once conducted to the scaffold.

11. On reaching the scaffold the procedure will be as follows:–

a. The executioner will:-
i. Place the culprit exactly under the part of the beam to which the rope is attached.
ii. Put the white linen cap on the culprit.
iii. Put on the rope round the neck quite tightly (with the cap between the rope and the neck), the metal eye being directed forwards, and placed in front of the angle of the lower jaw, so that with the constriction of the neck it may come underneath the chin. The noose should be kept tight by means of a stiff leather washer, or an india-rubber washer, or a wedge.

b. While the executioner is carrying out the procedure in paragraph (a) the assistant executioner will:-
i. Strap the culprit's legs tightly.
ii. Step back beyond the white safety line so as to be well clear of the trap doors.
iii. Give an agreed visual signal to the executioner to show that he is clear.

c. On receipt of the signal from his assistant the executioner will:-
i. Withdraw the safety pin.
ii. Pull the lever which lets down the trap doors.

13. The body [3] will [4] be carefully raised from the pit, provided [5] the

14. [] provided that the Medical Officer declares life to be extinct. Then the body will be detached from the rope and removed to the place set aside for the Coroner's inspection, a careful record having first been made and given to the Medical Officer of both the initial and final drops. The rope will be removed from the neck, and also the straps from the body. In laying out the body for the inquest, the head will be raised three inches by placing a small piece of wood under it.

[notes in original manuscript copy]

1. Manual insertion: "THEN"
2. Struck through and replaced by "provided": "as soon as"

3. Manual insertion: "WILL HANG FOR A MINIMUM OF 45 MINUTES"

4. The underlined words are struck through in the typescript. Manually inserted instead: "twine wrapped round".

5. Page 1 of the document ends here in the facsimile. The missing part of the sentence is probably: "be then raised from the pit, and disconnected from the rope."

---

[1] Manual insertion: "THEN"

[2] Struck through and replaced by "provided": "as soon as"

[3] Manual insertion: "WILL HANG FOR A MINIMUM OF 45 MINUTES"

[4] The underlined words are struck through in the typescript. Manually inserted instead: "twine wrapped round".

[5] Page 1 of the document ends here in the facsimile. The missing part of the sentence is probably: "be then raised from the pit, and disconnected from the rope."

BIBLIOGRAPHY

BOOKS:

Abbott, G., *Execution: The Guillotine, the Pendulum, the Thousand Cuts, the Spanish Donkey, and 66 Other Ways of Putting Someone to Death* (St. Martins 2005)

Abbott, G., *The Book of Execution* (Headline 1994)

Baddeley, Alan, *Human Memory: Theory and Practice* (Psychology Press 1997)

Bailey, B., *Hangmen of England* (Barnes & Noble 1989)

Banks, S., *The British Execution* (Shire 2013)

Banner, S., *The Death Penalty: An American History* (Harvard 2002)

Beccaria, C., *An Essay on Crimes and Punishments* (International Pocket Library 1983)

Bedau, H., Cassell, P., *Debating the Death Penalty* (Oxford 2004)

Christianson, S., *The Last Gasp: The Rise and Fall of the American Gas Chamber* (U. California 2010)

Clark, J. G., et al., *Biomechanics of the Craniovertebral Junction*, in Klika, V., ed., *Biomechanics in Application* (Intech 2011)

Compilation, *The Bill of Rights* (Applewood Press [1791])

Conot, R. E., *Justice at Nuremberg* (Carroll & Graf 1983)

Costanza, M., *Just Revenge: Costs and Consequences of the Death Penalty* (St. Martins 2001)

Dow, D. R., Dow, M., *The Machinery of Death: The Reality of America's Death Penalty Regime* (Routledge 2002)

Duff, C., A *Handbook of Hanging* (NYRB 2001)

Edlich, R. F., et al., *Modern Concepts of Treatment and Prevention of Electrical Burns* (J Long Term Eff Med Implants. 5(5) 2005)

Eds., *Hanging* (Encyclopaedia Britannica v. XIII, p. 911 1910)

Engel, H., *Lord High Executioner: an Unabashed Look at Hangmen, Headsmen, and Their Kind* (Firefly Book 1996)

Evans, K. M., *Capital Punishment: Cruel and Unusual?* (Information Plus 2012)

Flanders, F.A., *Capital Punishment* (Facts on File 1991)

Garrido, M. M., Bayarri, J. G., *Hypoxic Encephalopathy*, in Tanasecu, R., ed., *Miscellanes on Encephalopathies* (In Tech 2012)

Gatrell, V. A. C., *The Hanging Tree: Execution and the English People 1770-1868* (Oxford 1996)

Ghonheim, M. M., *Awareness During Anesthesia* (Butterworth-Heinemann 2001)

Gonzalez-Day, K., *Lynching in the West 1850-1935* (Duke 2006)

Graeber, C., *The Good Nurse* (Twelve Hatchette 2013)

Grossman, M., *Encyclopedia of Capital Punishment* (ABC-CLIO 1998)

Henderson, H., *Capital Punishment* (Facts on File 2006)

Hill, C., *The World Turned Upside Down: Radical Ideas During the English Revolution* (Penguin 1991)

Hoffer, P. C., *The Salem Witchcraft Trials: A Legal History* (U. Kansas 1997)

Holmes, O. W., *The Common Law* (Holmes Press 2012)

Kaufman-Osborn, T. V., *From Noose to Needle* (U. Michigan 2005)

Köff-Maier, P., ed., Wolff-Heidegger: *The Color Atlas of Human Anatomy* (Sterling 2004)

Koumbourlis, A. C., *Electrical Injuries* (Crit Care Med. Nov: 30(11 Suppl) 2002)

Lane, B., *The Encyclopedia of Cruel and Unusual Punishment* (True Crime 1993)

Laurence, J., *The History of Capital Punishment* (Citadel 1960)

Lemann, N., *Redemption: The Last Battle of the Civil War* (Tantor Media 2006)

Levy, L. W., *Origins of the Bill of Rights* (Yale 2001)

Madison, A., *Vigilantism in America* (Seabury Press 1973)

Marquart, J. W., et al., *The Rope, the Chair, & the Needle: Capital Punishment in Texas 1923-1990* (U. Texas 1994)

Masur, Louis P., *Rites of Execution: Capital Punishment and the Transformation of American Culture 1776-1865* (Oxford 1989)

Maurus, M. R., *The Nuremburg War Crimes Trial 1945-1946* (Bedford/St. Martins 1997)

Moses, N. H., *Lynching and Vigilantism in the United States: An Annotated Bibliography* (Greenwood 1997)

Mostofi, S. B., *Fracture Classifications in Clinical Practice* (Springer 2006)

Persico, J. E., *Nuremberg: Infamy on Trial* (Penguin 1994)

Pincus, S. C. A., *England's Glorious Revolution 1688-1689* (Bedford/St. Martins 2006)

Plucknett, T. F. T., *A Concise History of the Common Law* (Liberty Fund 2010)

Shuler, J., *The Thirteenth Turn: A History of the Noose* (Public Affairs 2014)

Stassen, G. H., ed., *Capital Punishment: A Reader* (Pilgrim 1998)

Steelwater, Eliza, *The Hangman's Knot: Lynching, Legal Execution, and America's Struggle with the Death Penalty* (Westview Press 2003)

Suchomel, P., et al., *Reconstruction of Upper Cervical Spine and Craniovertebral Junction* {Ch. 12.1} (Springer 2011)

Vila, B., Morris, C., eds., *Capital Punishment in the United States: A Documentary History* (Greenwood 1997)

Webb, S., *Execution: A History of Capital Punishment in Britain* (The History Press 2011)

Wilson, R. M., *Encyclopedia of Murder & Execution in the Wild West* (RaMA Press 2006)

PERIODICALS & PAPERS

Aberdere, Lord, Chair., *Minutes of Evidence, Examination of Rev. S. Haughton, MD* (Home Office Committee of Inquiry: The Execution of Capital Sentences 16 March 1886)

Alboni, P., et al., *An Abnormal Neural Reflex Plays a Role in Causing Syncope in Sinus Bradycardia* (J. Am. Coll. Cardiol. Oct: 22(4) 1993)

AlBuhairan, F., et al., *Non-suicidal Self-strangulation among Adolescents in Saudi Arabia: Case Series of the Choking Game* (J Forensic Leg Med. Feb: 30:45 2015)

Ambade, V. N., et al., *Suicidal and Homicidal Deaths: A Comparative and Circumstantial Approach* (J. Forensic Leg. Med. Jul: 14(5) 2007)

Annas, G. J., *Toxic Tinkering- Lethal-injection Execution and the Constitution* (Oct: 359(14) 2008)

Annas, G. J., *Killing with Kindness: Why the FDA Need not Certify Drugs Used for Execution Safe and Effective* (Am. J. Public Health Sep: 75(9) 1985)

Annas, G. J., *Nurses and the Death Penalty* (Nurs. Law Ethics May: 1(5) 1980)

Anzellotti, F., et al., *Autoscopic Phenomena: Case Report and Review of Literature* (Behav Brain Funct. Jan:7(1):2 2011)

Asensio, J. A., et al., *One Hundred Five Penetrating Cardiac Injuries: a 2-year Prospective Evaluation* (J Trauma. Jun: 44(6) 1998)

Arslan, M. N., et al., *Possible Death Mechanisms Other than Respiratory Asphyxia in a Suicidal Hanging Case* (Rom. J. Leg. Med. 21 2013)

Barbería-Marcalain, E., et al., *The Choking Game: a Potentially Lethal Game* (An Pediatr (Barc). Nov: 73(5) 2010)

Badkur, D.S., et al., *Nomenclature for Knot Position in Hanging: A Study of 200 Cases* (J Indian Acad Forensic Med. Jan- March: 34/1 2012)

Baumann, A., et al., *The Ethical and Legal Aspects of Palliative Sedation in Severely Brain-injured Patients: a French Perspective* (Philos Ethics Humanit Med. Feb: 6:4 2011)

Behrendt, N., et al., *The Lethal Paraphiliac Syndrome: Accidental Autoerotic Deaths in Four Women and a Review of the Literature* (Int J Legal Med. Jun: 116(3) 2002)

Benditt, D. G., et al. *Review Article: Heart Rate and Blood Pressure Control in Vasovagal Syncope* (J. Interv. Card. Electrophysiol. Mar: 2(1) 1998)

Bischoff, P., et al., *Undesired Awareness Phenomena During General Anesthesia : Evidence-based State of Knowledge, Current Discussions and Strategies for Prevention and Management* (Anaesthesist. Oct: 64(10) 2015)

Bishop, J. P., *Euthanasia, Efficiency, and the Historical Distinction Between Killing a Patient and Allowing a Patient to Die* (J Med Ethics. Apr: 32(4) 2006)

Blanchette, C. M., et al., *Economic Burden in Direct Costs of Concomitant Chronic Obstructive Pulmonary Disease and Asthma in a Medicare Advantage Population* (Manag Care Pharm. Mar: 14(2) 2008)

Bleecker, M. L., *Carbon Monoxide Intoxication* (Handb Clin Neurol. 131 2015)

Boghossian, E, et al., *Respiratory, Circulatory, and Neurological Responses to Hanging: A Review of Animal Models* (J. Forensic Sci. Sep: 55(5) 2010)

Breitmeier, D., et al., *Accidental Autoerotic Deaths Between 1978 and 1997. Institute of Legal Medicine, Medical School Hannover* (Forensic Sci Int. Oct:137(1) 2003)

Brock, D. W., *Euthanasia* (Yale J Biol Med. Mar: 65(2) 1992)

Bruce, A., Boston, P., *Relieving Existential Suffering Through Palliative Sedation: Discussion of an Uneasy Practice* (J Adv Nurs. Dec: 67(12) 2011)

Byard, R. W., et al., *a Comparison of Typical Death Scene Features in Cases of Fatal Male and Autoerotic Asphyxia with a Review of the Literature* (Forensic Sci Int. Dec: 48(2) 1990)

Candelario-Jalil, E., *Injury and Repair Mechanisms in Ischemic Stroke: Considerations for the Development of Novel Neurotherapeutics* (Curr Opin Investig Drugs. Jul;10(7) 2009)

Cassell, E. J., Rich B. A., *Intractable End-of-life Suffering and the Ethics of Palliative Sedation* (Pain Med. Mar:11(3) 2010)

Center for Disease Control (U.S.),"Choking Game" Awareness and Participation among 8th Graders--oregon, 2008 (Morb Mortal Wkly Rep. Jan: 59(1) 2010)

Center for Disease Control (U.S.), Unintentional Strangulation Deaths from the "Choking Game" among Youths Aged 6-19 Years--united States, 1995-2007 (Morb Mortal Wkly Rep. Feb: 57(6) 2008)

Chakravarty, A. , Kapoor, P., Concepts and Debates in End-of-life Care (Indian J Med Ethics Jul-Sep;9(3) 2012)

Clarke, G., et al., Withdrawal of Anticancer Therapy in Advanced Disease: a Systematic Literature Review (BMC Cancer. Nov: 15(1) 2015)

Clément, R., et al., Fracture of the Neck Structures in Suicidal Hangings: a Retrospective Study on Contributing Variables (Forensic Sci Int. Apr: 15;207 2011)
Clément, R., et al., Mechanism of Death in Hanging: A Historical Review of the Evolution of Pathophysiological Hypotheses (J. Forensic Sci. Sep: 55(5) 2010)

Colbourne, F., et al., Electron Microscope Evidence Against Apoptosis as the Mechanism of Neuronal Death in Global Ischemia (J. Neurosci. June: 19(11) 1999)

Collins, N., et al., End of Life in ICU- Care of the Dying or 'Pulling the Plug' (Ir. Med. J. Apr: 99(4) 2006)

Connor, Tracey, Firing Squad to Gas Chamber: How Long Do Executions Take? (NBC News March 25, 2015)

Cooper, M. A., Emergent Care of Lightning and Electrical Injuries (Semin Neurol. Sep;15(3) 1995)

Cothren, C.C., et al., Cervical Spine Fracture Patterns Predictive of Blunt Vertebral Artery Injury (J. Trauma Nov: 55(5) 2003)

Cristen, A. J., Alfred P. Southwick, MDS, DDS: Dental Practitioner, Educator and Originator of Electrical Executions (J Hist Dent. Nov;48(3) 2000)

Curfman, G. D., et al., *Physicians and Execution* (N Engl J Med. Jan: 358(4) 2008)

Davenney, E., Neale, H., Forbes, R. B., *A Systematic Review of Cases of Sudden and Severe Headache (Thunderclap Headache): Should Lists Be Evidence Based?* (J. Headache Pain 15/49 2014)

Dawson, V.L., Dawson T.M., *Deadly Conversations: Nuclear-Mitochondrial Cross-talk* (J. Bioenerg. Biomembr. Aug:36(4) 2004)

Degiannis, E., et al., *Penetrating Cardiac Injuries: Recent Experience in South Africa* (World J Surg. Jul: 30(7) 2006)

Denno, D. W., *The Lethal Injection Quandary: How Medicine has Dismantled the Death Penalty* (Ford. Law R. Oct: 76(1) 2007)

Dokov, W., *Electrocution-related Mortality: a Review of 351 Deaths by Low-voltage Electrical Current* (Ulus Travma Acil Cerrahi Derg. Mar;16(2) 2010)

Donatelli, L. A., et al., *Ethical Issues in Critical Care and Cardiac Arrest: Clinical Research, Brain Death and Organ Donation* (Semin. Neurol. Sep: 26(4) 2006)

Drought, T. S., Koenig, B.A., *"Choice" in End-of-life Decision Making: Researching Fact or Fiction?* (Gerontologist. Oct: 42 Spec No 3 2002)

Eisenchlas, J. H., *Palliative Sedation* (Curr Opin Support Palliat. Care Oct:1(3) 2007)

Emanuel, E. J., Battin M. P., *What Are the Potential Cost Savings from Legalizing Physician-assisted Suicide?* (N Engl J Med. Jul: 339(3) 1998)

Emanuel, E. J., *Cost Savings at the End of Life. What Do the Data Show?* (JAMA. Jun: 275(24) 1996)

Enomoto, L. M., et al., *The Cost of Hospice Services in Terminally Ill Patients With Head and Neck Cancer* (JAMA Otolaryngol Head Neck Surg. Oct 8:1-9. 2015)

Errando, C. L., et al., *Awareness with Recall During General Anaesthesia: a Prospective Observational Evaluation of 4001 Patients* (Br J Anaesth. Aug:101(2) 2008)

Fassett, D. R., et al., *Vertebral Injuries Associated with Cervical Spine Injuries: A Review of the Literature* (J. Spinal. Disord. Tech. Jun: 21(4) 2008)

Ferner, R. E., *Post-Mortem Clinical Pharmacology* (Br. Med. J. Clin. Pharm. 66(4) 2008)

Ferro, F. P., et al., *Traumatic Spondylolisthesis of the Axis: Epidemiology, Management and Outcome* (Acta Orlop Bras 20(2) 2012)

Fineschi, V., et al., *Cardiac Pathology in Death from Electrocution* (Int J Legal Med. Mar: 120(2) 2006)

Fischer, C., Mutschler, V., *Traumatic Brain Injuries in Adults: from Coma to Wakefulness. Neurophysiological Data* (Ann Readapt Med Phys. Nov: 45(8) 2002)

Fish, R, *Electric Shock, Part II: Nature and Mechanisms of Injury* (J Emerg Med. Jul-Aug: 11(4) 1993)

Fontanarosa, P. B., *Electrical Shock and Lightning Strike* (Ann Emerg Med. Feb: 22(2 Pt 2) 1993)

Forbes, C., et al., *A Rapid and Systematic Review of the Clinical Effectiveness and Cost-effectiveness of Topotecan for Ovarian Cancer* (Health Technol Assess. 5(28) 2001)

Förster, J. G., *Short-acting Spinal Anesthesia in the Ambulatory Setting* (Curr Opin Anaesthesiol. Dec: 27(6) 2014)

Förster, J. G., Rosenberg, P. H., *Revival of Old Local Anesthetics for Spinal Anesthesia in Ambulatory Surgery* (Curr Opin Anaesthesiol. Dec: 24(6) 2011)

French, C. C., *Near-death Experiences in Cardiac Arrest Survivors* (Prog Brain Res. 150 2005).

Friedman, D., et al., *Vertebral Artery Injury After Acute Cervical Spine Trauma: Rate of Occurence as Detected by MR Angiography and Assessment of Clinical Consequences* (Am. J. Roentgenol. Feb: 164(2) 1995)

Fujikawa, D. G., *The Role of Excitotoxic Programmed Necrosis in Acute Brain Injury* (Comp. & Structural Biotech. J. 13 2015)

Garland, P. V., *History of Military Executions* (Military Police 19:14-2 Fall 2014)

Garrido, M. M., et al., *Quality of Life and Cost of Care at the End of Life: the Role of Advance Directives* (. J Pain Symptom Manage. May: 49(5) 2015)

Gill, J. R., *Suicide by Cyanide: 17 Deaths* (J Forensic Sci. Jul: 49(4) 2004)

Groner, J., *Lethal Injection: A Stain on the Face of Medicine* (Br. Med. J. Nov: 325(7371) 2002)

Guidet, B., et al., *The Durban World Congress Ethics Round Table Conference Report: II. Withholding or Withdrawing of Treatment in Elderly Patients Admitted to the Intensive Care Unit* (J Crit Care. Dec: 29(6) 2014)

Guérit, J. M., *Medical Technology Assessment Eeg and Evoked Potentials in the Intensive Care Unit* (Neurophysiol Clin.Sep: 29(4) 1999)

Hamber, E. A., Viscomi, C. M., *Intrathecal Lipophilic Opioids as Adjuncts to Surgical Spinal Anesthesia* (Reg Anesth Pain Med. May: 24(3) 1999)

Harsharvardhana, N. S., Dabke, H. V., *Risk Factors for Vertebral Artery Injuries in Cervical Spine Trauma* (Othop. Rev (Pavia) Oct: 6(3) 2014)

Hellier, C., Connolly, R., *Cause of Death in Judicial Hanging: A Review and Case Study* (Med. Sci. Law Jan:49(1) 2009)

Hemphill, J. C. 3rd, White, D. B., *Clinical Nihilism in Neuroemergencies* (Emerg Med Clin North Am. Feb:27(1) 2009)

Hernandez-Meza, G., et al., Near-Infrared Spectroscopy for the Evaluation of Anesthetic Depth (Biomed Res Int. 2015:939418 2015)

Hillman, H., *The Possible Pain Experienced During Execution by Different Methods* (Perception 22(6) 1993)

Hirano, S., et al., *Responses of Cerebral Blood Volume and Oxygenation to Carotid Ligation and Hypoxia in Young Rabbits: Near-infrared Spectroscopy Study* (J. Child. Neurol. Jul: 8(3) 1993)

Hou, Y., et al., *Infrequent near Death Experiences in Severe Brain Injury Survivors - a Quantitative and Qualitative Study* (Ann Indian Acad Neurol. Jan: 16(1) 2013)

Hughes, M. T., Smith, T. J., *The Growth of Palliative Care in the United States* (Annu Rev Public Health. 35 2014)

Jackson, R. S., et al., *Upper Cervical Spine Injuries* (J. Am. Ac. Orth Sur. Jul: 10(4) 2002)

James, R., Nasmyth-Jones, R., *The Occurrence of Cervical Fractures in Victims of Judicial Hanging* (J. Forensic Sci. Apr:54(1) 1992)

James, T. N., et al., *Cardiac Abnormalities Demonstrated Postmortem in Four Cases of Accidental Electrocution and Their Potential Significance Relative to Nonfatal Electrical Injuries of the Heart* (Am Heart J. Jul;120(1) 1990)

Janssen, W., et al., *Forensic Aspects of 40 Accidental Autoerotic Deaths in Northern Germany* (Forensic Sci Int. Jan: 147 Suppl:S61-4 2005)

Jayaprakash S., Sreekumari K., *Pattern of Injuries to Neck Structures in Hanging- An Autopsy Study* (Am. J. Forensic Med. Pathol. Dec; 33(4) 2012)

Japaridze, N., et al., *Neuronal Networks During Burst Suppression as Revealed by Source Analysis* (PLoS One. Apr:10(4) 2015)

Jha, M. K., et al., *Judicial Hanging- Cause of Death* (J. Punjab. Ac. Forensic Med. Tox. Dec: 12(2) 2012)

Johnson, K., *A Moral Dilemma: Killing and Letting Die* (Br J Nurs. Jun: 2(12) 1993)

Jox, R.J., et al., *End-of-life Decisions, Powers of Attorney, and Advance Directives* (Nervenarzt. Jun:79(6) 2008)

Ju, Y. S., Schwedt, T. J., *Abrupt-Onset Severe Headache* (Semin. Neurol. Ap: 30(2) 2010)

Kadlac, A., *Flouting the Demands of Justice? Physician Participation in Execution* (J. Med. Philos. Oct: 39(5) 2014)

Kahane, G., Savulescu, J., *Brain Damage and the Moral Significance of Consciousness* (J Med Philos. Feb: 4(1) 2009)

Kaplan, J., et al., *Centerfire Frangible Ammunition: Wounding Potential and Other Forensic Concerns* (Am J Forensic Med Pathol. Dec:19(4) 1998)

Kao, L. W., Nañagas, K. A., *Carbon Monoxide Poisoning* (Emerg Med Clin North Am. Nov: 22(4) 2004)

Karger, B., *Electrocution– Autopsy Study with Emphasis on "Electrical Petechiae"* (Forensic Sci Int. May:126(3) 2002)

Karger, B., *Penetrating Gunshots to the Head and Lack of Immediate Incapacitation. I. Wound Ballistics and Mechanisms of Incapacitation* (Int J Legal Med. 108(2) 1995)

Keane, M., *The Ethical "Elephant" in the Death Penalty "Room"* (Am. J. Bioeth. Oct: 8(10) 2008)

Kenny, R. A., et al., *Autonomic Reflexes in Patients with Cardioinhibitory Carotid Sinus Syncope* (Clin. Auton. Res. Apr: 3(2) 1993)

Khan A., Leventhal R. M., *Medical Aspects of Capital Punishment: Executions* (J Forensic Sci. Jul;47(4) 2002)

Khokhlov, V.D.

-a) *Pressure on the Neck Calculated for any Point Along the Ligature* (Forensic Sci. Int. Dec:123(2-3) 2001)

-b) *Calculation of Tension Exerted on a Ligature in Incomplete Hanging* (Forensic Sci. Int. Dec:123(2-3) 2001)

Kinoshita, H., *Pathology of Spinal Cord Injuries Due to Fracture and Fracture-Dislocation of the Cervical Spine* (Paraplegia 32 1994)

Kobayashi, K., et al., *Fatal Case of Cervical Blunt Vascular Injury with Cervical Vertebral Fracture: A Case Report* (Nagoya J. Med. Sci. Aug: 77(3) 2015)

Koenig, M. A., et al., *Clinical Neurophysiologic Monitoring and Brain Injury from Cardiac Arrest* (Neurol Clin. Feb: 24(1) 2006)

Komenda, J., et al., *Forensic and Clinical Issues in the Use of Frangible Projectile* (J Forensic Leg Med. Aug: 20(6) 2013)

Koniaris, L. G., et al., *Ethical Implications of Modifying Lethal Injection Protocols* (PLoS Med. Jun: 5(6) 2008)

Koniaris, L. G., et al., *Inadequate Anaesthesia in Lethal Injection for Execution*.(Lancet.Apr: 16-22 2005)

Kopelman, *Conceptual and Moral Disputes about Futile and Useful Treatments* (J Med Philos. Apr: 20(2) 1995)

Krijnen, P. A., et al., *Apoptosis in Myocardial Ishaemia and Infarction* (J. Clin. Pathol. Nov:55(11) 2002)

Lateef, W. M., et al., *Penetrating Cardiac Injury: a Review* (Trauma Mon. Spring: 17(1) 2012)

Lebl, D. R., et al., *Vertebral Artery Injury Associated with Blunt Cervical Spine Trauma: A Multivariate Regression Analysis* (Spine Jul: 38(16) 2013)

Lesieur, O., et al., *Withholding or Withdrawal of Treatment Under the French Rules: A Study Performed in 43 Intensive Care Units* (Ann. Intensive Care Dec; 5(1) 2015)

Leys, D., et al., *Cervical Artery Dissection* (Eur. Neurol. 37(1) 1997)

Li, D., et al., *Asphyxia-activated Corticocardiac Signaling Accelerates Onset of Cardiac Arrest* (Proc Natl Acad Sci U S A. Apr: 112(16) 2015)

Li, M., Hamilton, W., *Review of Autopsy Findings in Judicial Electrocutions* (Am. J. Med. Pathol. Sep:26(3) 2005)

Linn, F. H., *Primary Thunderclap Headache* (Handb Clin Neurol. 97 2010)

Lo, W. K., Chong, J. L., Chen, L. H., *Combined Spinal Epidural for Labour Analgesia– Duration, Efficacy and Side Effects of Adding Sufentanil or Fentanyl to Bupivacaine Intrathecally vs Plain Bupivacaine* (Singapore Med J. Oct: 40(10 1999)

Longstreth, W. T., et al., *Hangman's Fracture* (J Neurosurg. Spine Nov: 15(5) 2011)

Lotto, L., et al., *Attitudes Towards End-of-life Decisions and the Subjective Concepts of Consciousness: an Empirical Analysis* (PLoS One. 7(2) 2012)

Luchetti, M., *Eluana Englaro, Chronicle of a Death Foretold: Ethical Considerations on the   Recent Right-to-die Case in Italy* (J Med Ethics. Jun: 36(6) 2010)

Maiden, N., *Ballistics Reviews: Mechanisms of Bullet Wound Trauma* (Forensic Sci Med Pathol. 5(3) 2009)

Manchikanti, L., et al., *Saga of Payment Systems of Ambulatory Surgery Centers for Interventional Techniques: an Update* (Pain Physician. Mar-Apr;15(2) 2012)

Manchikanti, L., Boswell, M.V., *Interventional Techniques in Ambulatory Surgical Centers: a Look at the New Payment System* (Pain Physician. Sep;10(5) 2007)

Martin, L. J., et al., *Neurodegeneration In Excitology, Global Cerebral Ischemia, and Target Deprivation: A Perspective on the Contributions of Apoptosis and Necrosis* (Brain Res. Bull. Jul:46(4) 1998)

Masood, U. R., et al., *Limiting Intensive Care Therapy in Dying Critically Ill Patients: Experience From a Tertiary Care Center in United Arab Emirates* (Int. J. Crit. Illn. Inj. Sci. Jul: 3(3) 2013)

Matharu, et al., *Thunderclap Headache: an Approach to a Neurologic Emergency* (Curr Neurol Neurosci Rep. Mar;7(2) 2007)

Matsunaga, S., Shuto, T., *Long-term Outcomes of Gamma Knife Surgery for Posterior Fossa Arteriovenous Malformations* (Neurol Med Chir (Tokyo) 54(10) 2014)

Mogilka, S. M., *The Entire Life: Nursing's Obligation to Bring Truth to the Death Penalty Debate* (Nurs. Forum Jan: 32(1) 1997)

Morgan, B., et al., *Adult Post-Mortem Imaging in Traumatic and Cardiorespiratory Death and its Relation to Clinical Radiological Imaging* (Br. J. Radiol. 87 20130662 2014)

Morita, T., *Ethical Validity of Palliative Sedation Therapy: A Multicenter, Prospective, Observational Study Conducted on Specialized Palliative Care Units in Japan* (J Pain Symptom Manage Oct;30(4) 2005)

Mueller, P. S., *The Terri Schiavo Saga: Ethical and Legal Aspects and Implications for Clinicians* (Pol Arch Med Wewn. Sep: 119(9) 2009)

Myers, W. C., et al., *The Relationship Between Serial Sexual Murder and Autoerotic Asphyxiation* (Forensic Sci Int. Apr: 176(2-3) 2008)

Nikoli, S., Zivkovi, V., *Cervical Spine Injuries in Suicidal Hanging Without Long-drop– Patterns and Possible Underlying Mechanisms of Injury: An Autopsy Study* (Forensic Sci. Med. Pathol. Jun: 10(2) 2014)

Oehmichen, M., et al., *Gunshot Injuries to the Head and Brain Caused by Low-velocity Handguns and Rifles. A Review* (Forensic Sci Int. Dec: 146(2-3) 2004)

Oehmichen, M., et al., *Brain Injury after Gunshot Wounding: Morphometric Analysis of Cell Destruction Caused by Temporary Cavitation* (J Neurotrauma Feb:17(2) 2000)

Ogoh, S., et al., *Carotid Baroreflex Function Ceases During Vasovagal Syncope* (Clin. Auton. Res. Feb: 14(1) 2004)

Olugbenga, A. E., *Modern Methods of Executing Condemned Prisoners: Elixir to Painful Killings?* (Int. J. Bus. Soc. Science Ap: 3(8) 2013)

Ortendahl, M., *Models Based on Value and Probability in Health Improve Shared Decision Making* (J Eval Clin Pract. Oct: 14(5) 2008)
Ortendahl, M., Fries, J. F., *Discounting and Risk Characteristics in Clinical Decision-making* (Med Sci Monit. Mar: 12(3) 2006)

Padela, A., Mohiuddin, A., *Ethical Obligations and Clinical Goals in End-of-life Care: Deriving a Quality-of-life Construct Based on the Islamic Concept of Accountability Before God* (Am J Bioeth.15(1) 2015)

Padrta, J. C. Jr., et al., *Expanding Handgun Bullets* (J Trauma. 1997 Sep: 43(3) 1997)

Pankratz, H., et al., *Decapitation by Hanging* (Arch Kriminol. Nov-Dec;178(5-6) 1986)

Panksepp, .J., et al., *Does Any Aspect of Mind Survive Brain Damage That Typically Leads to a Persistent Vegetative State? Ethical Considerations* (Philos Ethics Humanit Med. Dec: 2:32 2007)

Parent, A. D., et al., *Lateral Cervical Spine Dislocation and Vertebral Artery Injury* (Neurosurgery Sep: 31(3) 1992)

Payne, K., et al., *The Heath Economics of Palliative Care* (Oncology (Williston Park) Jun:16(6) 2002)

Pierson, D. J., *Pathophysiology and Clinical Effects of Chronic Hypoxia* (Resp. Care Jan: 45(1) 2000)

Pierrepoint, A., *Executioner: Pierrepoint* (Verulam 2005)

Pollak, S., *Pathomorphological Constellation in Death Resulting from High Voltage Electricity*
(Arch Kriminol.165(1-2) 1980)

Pollanen, M. S., *Subtle Fatal Manual Neck Compression* (Med. Sci. Law Ap: 41(2) 2001)

Pollock, J. E., *Neurotoxicity of Intrathecal Local Anaesthetics and Transient Neurological Symptoms* (Best Pract Res Clin Anaesthesiol. Sep:17(3) 2003)

Prockop, L. D., Chichkova, R. I., *Carbon Monoxide Intoxication: an Updated Review* (J Neurol Sci. Nov: 262(1-2) 2007)

Quan, K. J., et al., *Mechanisms of Heart Rate and Arterial Blood Pressure Control: Implications for the Pathophysiology of Neurocardiaogenic Syncope* (Pacing Clin. Electrophysiol. Mar: 20(3) 1997)

Quinn, K. P., *Assisted Suicide and Equal Protection: in Defense of the Distinction Between Killing and Letting Die* (Issues Law Med. Fall: 13(2) 1997)

Rabl, W., et al., *Hanging with Decapitation. Case Report–Biomechanics* (Arch Kriminol. Jan-Feb: 195(1-2) 1995)

Rady, M. Y., Verheijde, J. L., *Nonconsensual Withdrawal of Nutrition and Hydration in Prolonged Disorders of Consciousness: Authoritarianism and Rustworthiness in Medicine* (Philos Ethics Humanit Med. Nov: 9:16 2014)

Ragoschke-Schumm A et al., *Early Evaluation of Neurological Prognosis and Therapy after Cardiopulmonary Resuscitation: Current Opportunities and Clinical Implications* (Nervenarzt. Aug: 78(8) 2007)

Raub, J. A., Benignus, *Carbon Monoxide and the Nervous System* (Neurosci Biobehav Rev. Dec: 26(8) 2002)

Raub, J. A., et al., *Carbon Monoxide Poisoning--a Public Health Perspective* (Toxicology Apr: 7;145(1) 2000)

Rayes, M., et al., *Hangman's Fracture: A Historical and Biomechanical Perspective* (J. Neurosurg. Spine Feb: 14 2011)

Reay, D. T., et al., *Injuries Produced by Judicial Hanging. A Case Report* (Am J Forensic Med Pathol. Sep:15(3) 1994)

Reid, D., Gurwell, J., *Eyewitness: I Saw 189 Men Die in the Electric Chair* (Cordovan Press 1973)

Reynolds, A., *Executions and Hard Anglo-Saxon Justice* (Br. Arch. Mag. Feb: 31 1998)

Romain, M., Sprung, C. L., *End-of-Life Practices in the Intensive Care Unit: The Importance of Geography, Religion, Religious Affiliation and Culture* (Rambam Malmonides Med. J. Jan: 5(1) 2014)

Romanelli, F., *Lethal Injection as a Component of a Therapuetics Toxicology Module* (Am. J. Pharm. Ed. 75(6) 2011)

Romanelli, F., et al., *Issues Surrounding Lethal Injection as a Means of Capital Punishment* (Pharmacotherapy Dec: 28(12) 2008)

Rongchao, S., et al., *Pathological and Immunohistochemical Study of Lethal Primary Brain Stem Injuries* (Diag. Path. 7/54 2012)

Rosenblum, W., *Histopathologic Clues to the Pathways of Neuronal Death Following Ishemia/Hypoxia* (J. Neurotrauma May:14(5) 1997)

Rothschild, M. A, Schneider, V., *Decapitation as a Result of Suicidal Hanging* (Forensic Sci Int. Nov: ;106(1) 1999)
Sabermoghaddam, M., et al., *Survival After Judicial Hanging* (Am. J. Forensic Med. Pathol. Jun: 36(2) 2015)

Sanford, A., Gamelli, R. L., *Lightning and Thermal Injuries* (Handb Clin Neurol. 120 2014)

Santucci, R. A., Chang, Y. J., *Ballistics for Physicians: Myths about Wound Ballistics and Gunshot Injuries* (J Urol. Apr;171(4) 2004)

Sauvageau, A., *Current Reports on Autoerotic Deaths--five Persistent Myths* (Curr Psychiatry Rep. Jan: 16(1) 2014)

Sauvageau, A., *Autoerotic Deaths: a 25-year Retrospective Epidemiological Study* (Am J Forensic Med Pathol. Jun: 33(2) 2012)

Sauvageau, A., et al.:

-*a) Agonal Sequences in 14 Filmed Hangings With Comments on the Role of the Type of Suspension, Ischemic Habituation, and Ethanol Intoxication on the Timing of Agonal Responses* (Am. J. Forensic Med. Pathol. *in press* 2010)

-*b) Agonal Sequences in Eight Filmed Hangings: Analysis of Respiratory and Movement Responses to Asphyxia by Hanging* (J. Forensic Sci. Sep: 55(5) 2010)

Sauvaugeau, A., *Agonal Sequences in Four Filmed Hangings: Analysis of Respiratory and Movement Responses to Asphyxia by Hanging* (J. Forensic Sci. Jan:54(1) 2009)

Sauvageau, A., Racette, S., *Autoerotic Deaths in the Literature from 1954 to 2004: A Review* (J Forensic Sci. Jan: 51(1) 2006)

Sawaki K., Kawaguchi, M., *Some Correlations Between Procaine-induced Convulsions and Monoamines in the Spinal Cord of Rats* (Jpn J Pharmacol. Nov:51(3) 1989)

Schleicher, P., et al., *Traumatic Spondylolisthesis of the Axis Vertebra in Adults* (Global Spine J. Aug:5(4) 2015)

Schwedt, T. J., *Thunderclap Headache* (Continuum (Minneap Minn) Aug: 21(4 Headache) 2015)

Schwedt, T. J., Dodick, D. W., *Thunderclap Stroke: Embolic Cerebellar Infarcts Presenting as Thunderclap Headache* (Headache Mar;46(3) 2006)

Schwender, D., et al., *Awareness During General Anesthesia. Definition, Incidence, Clinical Relevance, Causes, Avoidance and Medicolegal Aspects* (Anaesthesist. Nov: 44(11) 1995)

Sharma, B. R., et al. , *Injuries to Neck Structures in Deaths Due to Constriction of Neck, With Special References to Hanging* (J. Forensic Leg. Med. Jul:15(5) 2008)

Schrag, B., et al., *Death Caused by Cardioinhibitory Reflex: What Experts Believe* (Am. J. Forensic Med. Pathol. Mar: 33(1) 2012)

Schrag, B., et al., *Death Caused by Cardioinhibitory Reflex: A Systematic Review of Cases* (Forensic Sci. Int. Apr: 15(207) 2011)

Sikora, A., Fleischman, A. R., *Physician Participation in Capital Punishment: A Question of Professional Integrity* (J. Urban Health Dec: 76(4) 1999)

Silver, D., *Lethal Injection, Autonomy and the Proper Ends of Medicine* (Bioethics. Apr:17(2) 2003)

Spence, M. W., et al., *Craniocervical Injuries in Judicial Hangings: An Anthropological Analysis of Six Cases* (Am. J. Forensic Med. Path. Dec: 20(4) 1999)

Sprung, C. L., et al., *Is the Patient's Right to Die Evolving into a Duty to Die?: Medical Decision Making and Ethical Evaluations in Health Care* (J Eval Clin Pract. 1997 Feb;3(1)

Stanley, J. M., et al., *The Appleton Consensus: Suggested International Guidelines for Decisions to Forego Medical Treatment* (J Med Ethics. Sep: 15(3) 1989)

Stein, R., *Group to Censure Physicians Who Play a Role in Lethal Injections* (Wash. Post Network News 5/2/2010) [Am. Board Anesthesiologists]

Stolls, M., *Heckler v. Chaney: Judicial and Administrative Regulation of Capital Punishment by Lethal Injection* (Am. J. Law Med. 11(2) 1985)

Sulmasy, D. P., *Managed Care and Managed Death* (Arch Intern Med. Jan 23:155(2) 1995)

Suárez-Peñaranda, J. M., et al., *Cardiac Inhibitory Reflex as a Cause/mechanism of Death* (J. Forensic Sci. Nov: 58(6) 2013)

Suárez-Peñaranda, J. M., et al., *Characterization of Lesions in Hanging Deaths* (J. Forensic Sci. May:53(3) 2008)

Tangka, F. K., et al., *End-of-life Medical Costs of Medicaid Cancer Patients* (Health Serv Res. Jun: 50(3) 2015)

Tappenden, P., et al., *Systematic Review and Economic Evaluation of Bevacizumab and Cetuximab for the Treatment of Metastatic Colorectal Cancer* (Health Technol Assess. Mar: 11(12) 2007)

Terazawa, K., et al., *A Bibliographic Discussion on the Obstruction of Arteries and Air Passage in Hanging* (Nihon Hoigaku Zasshi Aug: 45(4) 1991)

Thom, S. R., Keim, L. W., *Carbon Monoxide Poisoning: a Review Epidemiology, Pathophysiology, Clinical Findings, and Treatment Options Including Hyperbaric Oxygen Therapy* (J Toxicol Clin Toxicol. 27(3) 1989)

Thompson B.J., Ronaldson, P.T., *Drug Delivery to the Ischemic Brain* (Adv Pharmacol. Aug: 71 2014)

Tinkoff, G. H., O'Connor, R. E., *Validation of New Trauma Triage Rules for Trauma Attending Response to the Emergency Department* (J Trauma. Jun: 52(6) 2002)

Tominaga, G. T., et al., *Head Injuries in Hospital-admitted Adolescents and Adults with Skateboard-related Trauma* (Brain Inj. 29(9) 2015)

Tominaga, G. T., et al., *Epidemiological and Clinical Features of an Older High-risk Population of Skateboarders* (Injury. May: 44(5) 2012)

Toorop, R. J., et al., *Anatomy of the Carotid Sinus Nerve and Surgical Implications in Carotid Artery Syndrome* (J. Vasc. Surgery Jul: 50(1) 2009)

Töro, K, et al., *Incomplete Decapitation in Suicidal Hanging - Report of a Case and Review of the Literature.*(J Forensic Leg Med Apr:15(3) 2008)

Tsokos, M., et al., *Pathologic Features of Suicidal Complete Decapitations* (Forensic Sci Int. Jan: 139(2-3) 2004)

Urenholt, L., et al. *Fatal Subarachnoid Hemorrhage Associated with Internal Carotid Artery Dissection Resulting from Whiplash Trauma* (Forensic Sci. Med. Pathol. *in press* 2015)

Urmey, W. F., *Spinal Anaesthesia for Outpatient Surgery* (Best Pract Res Clin Anaesthesiol. Sep:17(3) 2003)

Uzün, I., et al., *Suicidal Hanging: Fatalities In Istanbul Retrospective Analysis of 761 Autopsy Cases* (J. Forensic Leg. Med. Oct: 14(7) 2007)

van Gijn, J., Rinkel, G., *Subarachnoid Haemorrhage: Diagnosis, Causes and Management* (Brain Feb:124(2) 2001)

Vadász, G., *Euthanasia and Other Decisions at the End of Life (Proposal for a More Transparent Terminology and Some Thoughts on the Legal Framework of Medical Treatment)* (Orv Hetil. Oct:151(43) 2010)

Wallace, S. K., et al., *Judicial Hanging: Postmortem Radiographic, CT, and MR Imaging Features with Autopsy Confirmation* (Radiology Oct:193(1) 1994)

West, R. R., et al., *Estimating Implied Rates of Discount in Healthcare Decision-making* (Health Technol Assess. 7(38) 2003)

Westover, M. B., et al., *The Human Burst Suppression Electroencephalogram of Deep Hypothermia* (Clin Neurophysiol. Oct;126(10) 2015)

Westover, M. B., et al., *Real-time Segmentation and Tracking of Brain Metabolic State in ICU EEG Recordings of Burst Suppression* (Conf Proc IEEE Eng Med Biol Soc. 2013)

Widgery, A., *Lethal Injection Under Fire: Drug Shortages and Court Challenges are Causing Lawmakers to Review Their Statess' Method of Execution* (State Legis. May: 41(5) 2015)

Wilkinson, D., *The Self-fulfilling Prophecy in Intensive Care* (Theor Med Bioeth. 30(6) 2009)

Jones, F. W., *The Examination of the Bodies of 100 Men Executed in Nubia in Roman Time* (Br Med J. Mar: 1(2465) 1908)

Yen, C. P., Steiner, L., *Gamma Knife Surgery for Brainstem Arteriovenous Malformations* (World NeurosurgJul: 76(1-2) 2011)

Yeo, S. S., Jang, S. H., *Delayed Neural Degeneration Following Gamma Knife Radiosurgery in a Patient with an Arteriovenous Malformation: a Diffusion Tensor Imaging Study* (Neuro Rehabilitation 31(2).2012)

Young, G. B., et al., *Anoxic-ischemic Encephalopathy: Clinical and Electrophysiological Associations with Outcome* (Neurocrit Care. 2(2) 2005)

Zivot, J. B., *The Absence of Cruelty is Not the Presence of Humanness: Physicians and the Death Penalty in the United States* (J. Philos. Ethics Hum. Med. (Dec: 7(13) 2012)

INDEX

*Stay Satan's hand where you can, it's already well
calloused by souls writhing in remorse.*